CW01081470

THE POSTCARD AGE

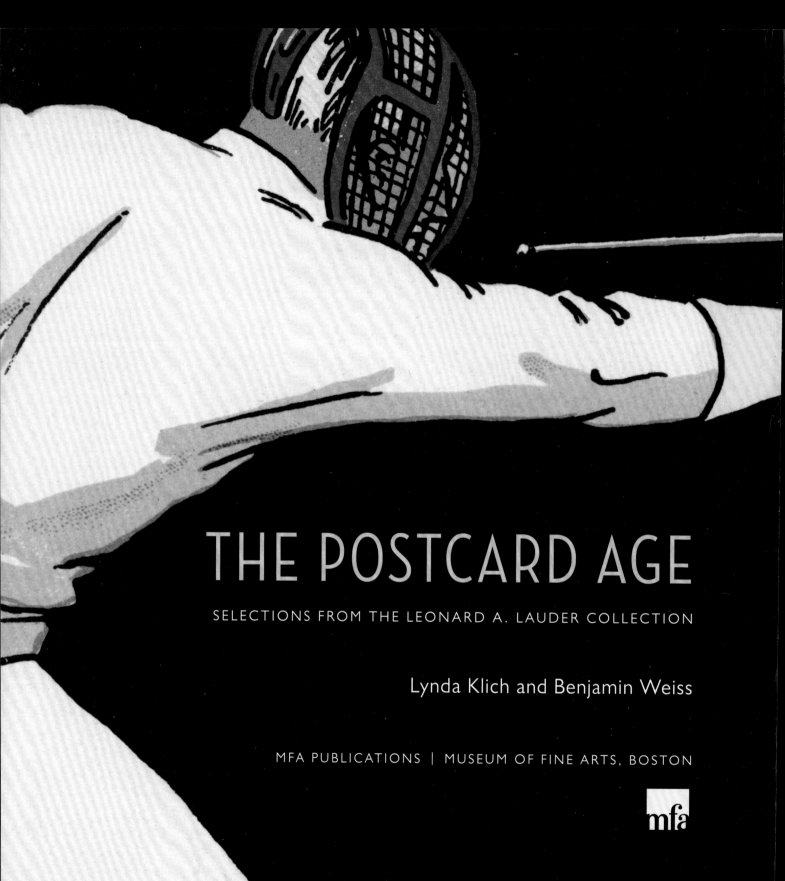

THE POSTCARD AGE

SELECTIONS FROM THE LEONARD A. LAUDER COLLECTION

Lynda Klich and Benjamin Weiss

MFA PUBLICATIONS | MUSEUM OF FINE ARTS, BOSTON

mfa

Grande Roue de
l'Exposition.

TO EVELYN H. LAUDER (1936–2011)

Wish you were here.

CONTENTS

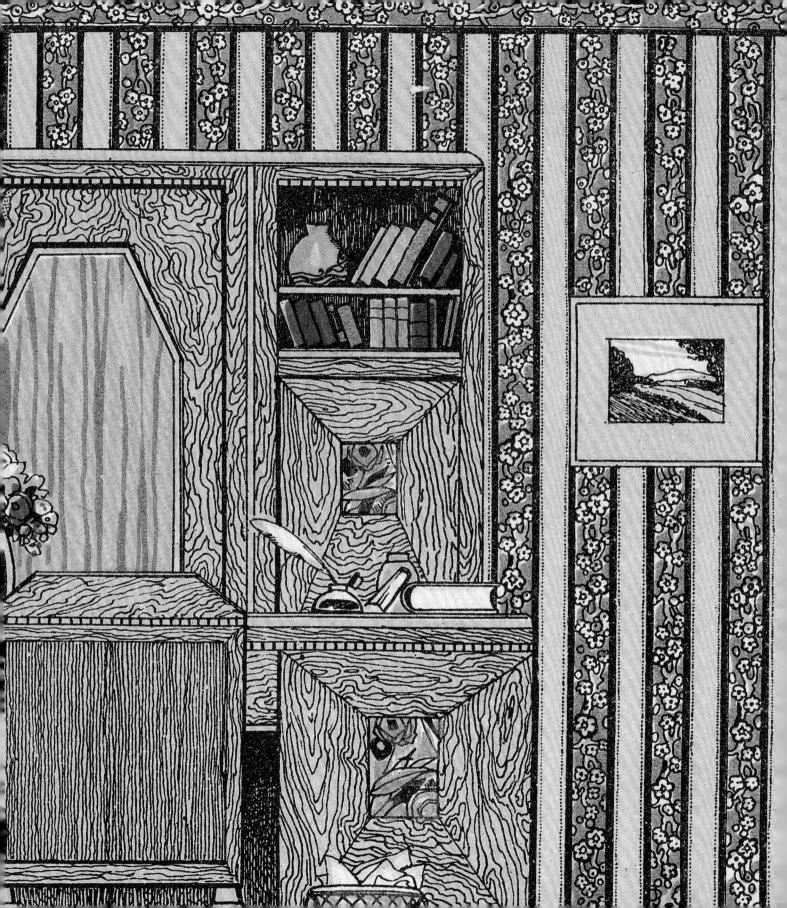

DIRECTOR'S FOREWORD

Great museums are born of great collectors. Any museum whose holdings have the depth, richness, or sheer audacity to make visitors pause and catch their breath has likely been the beneficiary of the unbridled enthusiasm of a driven private collector. The Museum of Fine Arts, Boston, has a number of such names in its history, individuals whose passions have, time and again, transformed the character of our collections.

Leonard A. Lauder is one such collector. Beginning with the gift of his Japanese postcards in 2002, and now with the even greater promise of his Western cards, which number about 100,000, he has shifted the center of gravity of the Museum's collection of works on paper. The two gifts are among the largest we have ever received, but they have also opened our eyes to objects of beauty and historical importance that had almost completely eluded our attention before.

We cannot know how a gift like the Lauder Archive will play out in the decades to come, for it is only with the passage of time and the attention of visitors and scholars that the collection will find its full meaning. Leonard Lauder, who has spent a lifetime building the collection, knows its secrets; but even his knowledge cannot predict what others will find and what connections they will make. For that is what institutions do: they provide the place where collections meet the world.

No single book or exhibition can do justice to an achievement as large and various as the Lauder Archive. Instead, *The Postcard Age* provides something akin to a tasting menu. Each of the sections here could be the nucleus of a book of its own. Some, in fact, may become so, for, like a tasting menu, this book is meant to lure readers and visitors back for much more in the years to come.

MALCOLM ROGERS
Ann and Graham Gund Director
Museum of Fine Arts, Boston

MESSAGES FROM THE POSTCARD AGE

LEONARD A. LAUDER

People often ask me, "Why postcards?" The answer is both easy and complex. At heart, my postcard collection represents excitement, pleasure, and adventure. It is hard to top the thrill of the chase, the satisfaction of finding a long-sought-after card, or the delight of discovering a new collecting category after all these years. Postcards also bring aesthetic enjoyment, a spark that comes from looking at an exceptionally well-designed object that brings together an artist's graphic ingenuity and individual style into a miniature masterpiece. When I look at a postcard from my collection today, I can often recall the first moment I held it in my hand, in a dealer's shop or at a postcard show. Each one takes me back over decades of collecting and ties together diverse aspects of my deeply personal engagement with art, design, and history.

At the same time, postcards open countless windows onto a broader collective past. An individual card makes a specific historical moment come alive in a vividly intimate way, whether it be the smartly clad figures in an illustrated advertisement that lured patrons into a busy turn-of-the-century Berlin café or a spectacular photograph that decades later captured the *Hindenburg*'s fiery end. The postcard bears witness to events, such as one series that chronicled the last moments of the life of Archduke Franz Ferdinand, before he was shot in Sarajevo on June 28, 1914. The last card of the series in my collection has a cross inked above the head of one of the assailants, conjuring up the card's original owner, who might have

marked it as if to say, "That's him—I saw him do it," before he sent it along to a friend [1]. The messages written on cards bring the past back to life as well, like "From Your Soldier Boy," an embroidered card sent from a young man in the trenches of the First World War to his sweetheart in England, "with best love from France" [2]. Postcards help remind us that history is lived and experienced by individuals.

Perhaps more important, as mass-produced multiples, postcards are what I consider "the best history lesson" about the time we are calling the Postcard Age. They record the technological, social, political, and artistic developments of the decades before and after World War I, a time when rapid and broad transformations shook the world. Postcards make tangible the excitement and novelty of the era's inventions, from new electrical products, like the lightbulb, that altered daily life, to even more astonishing ones, like the airplane, that permanently changed humanity's relationship with space and time. They make vivid what was at stake in the social and political issues of the early decades of the twentieth century, such as the alarm felt by those opposed to giving women the vote or the nationalist passions that united countries but ultimately fractured the Western world. These small pieces of card stock recall the excitement of the avant-garde, when artists used postcards to experiment with new styles and strategies. The Italian Futurists, for example, issued their own postcards to agitate for Italy's entrance into

1 The bomb-thrower Čabrinovič, 1914

2 Embroidered card, about 1915

the First World War. The artist Giacomo Balla then decorated one of these cards by hand and dedicated it to the Futurist leader F. T. Marinetti, pledging to be with him in his activist endeavors [3]. Like others experiencing the broader changes of the early twentieth century, such artists understood that the era's transformations necessitated completely new means of seeing, representing, and communicating. In short, postcards encapsulate the urgency of the past in a way that is impossible to contain in words.

But postcards did not just record or represent this dynamic era—they also participated actively in it. My collection contains a section entitled simply Postcard History, which includes cards depicting the history of the postcard industry, including production, dissemination, and collecting. These cards attest to the enormous popularity of postcards during the period that ran roughly from the mid-1890s to the First World War (though the postcard still remained an important visual and communications medium through the Second World War). During the craze, postcards were everywhere, sold in shops dedicated completely to them or by individual vendors on street corners. People clamored to buy the latest offerings from publishers who constantly fed the astronomical demand with novel formats or subjects.

Postcards generated such passion because they conveyed the exhilaration of the turn of the century. Postcards were fast, and postcards were new. When in 1869 the postal service of the Austro-Hungarian Empire began to issue cards that could go through the mail on their own, without envelopes, other nations quickly followed suit. By the 1890s, postcards had become an essential part of everyday life. They were the very cheapest things to mail—at half the price of a letter—and people did so with an enthusiasm verging on mania. Postcards were a seemingly instant communications technology—in some cities, a card mailed in the morning could reach its destination later that same day. They also offered an inexpensive way to communicate with loved ones who were far away. They even created new connections between like-minded aficionados of the new medium, who relied on fellow enthusiasts around the globe to help them build their own collections.

Postcards, which joined word and image, were just as up-to-date as the Internet is today. In fact, nearly every role the postcard played in the decades around 1900 has an analogue in the electronic technologies of the early twenty-first century. Just as today people issue invitations by e-mail, send quick messages by text, or share collections of images on Flickr, a hundred years ago they did the same things using the

3 The Futurist flag. March, don't rot; decorated by Giacomo Balla ("With you"), 1915; front and back

postcard. Postcards carried short notes about when visitors would arrive, messages about how much it might cost to paint a house, and orders for the goods and services pictured on their fronts. Whole businesses ran on postcards. The medium also spread the latest news, as photographers using film specially made to print directly on postcard stock could capture a key moment, print it right away, and immediately begin distributing the cards. Postcards thus offered pictorial records of the latest newsworthy events, whether global or local. At a time when telephones were used only on special occasions, movies were still a novelty, and newspapers were typically illustrated with line drawings rather than halftone photographs, postcards *were* new media. They allowed the current events and burning issues of the day to spread quickly and over long distances.

During the postcard craze, the industry was an important economic engine in many countries. For example, sixty factories employed more than twelve thousand people in Germany; and more than thirty thousand worked in the French industry.[1] Companies printed billions upon billions of postcards that would be bought, sold, sent, gathered into albums, stored in boxes, or played with by children. Taken together, the cards capture the dynamism of an age when people generally went out to be entertained

rather than having amusements beamed into their houses. They reflect every concern of the day and mirror the fashions, styles, and fads that flourished in the teeming new cities of the late nineteenth and early twentieth centuries—epitomized by Paris but echoed by towns large and small throughout Europe and the Americas. As a new form of communication that traveled quickly, postcards not only portrayed but also produced the excitement of the turn-of-the-century world.

The thrilling images of an era found on postcards and the suggestion of the urgent moment embodied by the medium are foremost among the reasons that I remained dedicated to collecting them for over half a century. My collection is inseparable from my life's experience. I have told of my long history with the postcard in previous publications about my Japanese and Wiener Werkstätte collections.[2] I have recalled my vivid childhood memories of the stunning postcards of New York City buildings that I bought at Woolworth's with my five-cent allowance; my first real collection, which contained postcards depicting the sleek and strikingly modern designs of Miami Beach's Art Deco buildings; and my teenage years as a charter member of the Metropolitan Postcard Club in New York. (I still have my original membership card, with number 75.) My early interest in post-

cards spurred other collections and interests, notably posters (I picked up original propaganda posters from the Office of War Information during World War II and stored them in my bathtub, much to my mother's chagrin). I also became a cinema buff, starting a film society at the University of Pennsylvania when I was a student there and organizing viewings of films such as *It Happened One Night* with Clark Gable and Claudette Colbert. For me, mass media—whether films, posters, or postcards—suggested exciting and immediate ways of seeing the world. I took a hiatus from these pursuits while I served in the U.S. Navy, married, and started a family with my beloved wife, Evelyn. In the mid-1960s, when I began to travel for the Estée Lauder Company as a young executive, I returned to the postcard, never having forgotten its hold on me. My new journeys took me around the globe. Postcards, I came to understand, could do the same. And they also let me go back in time.

In previous essays, I recounted developing a knowledge of and affinity for a particular type of card, whether Japanese or Viennese. Those cards—now at the Museum of Fine Arts, Boston, and promised to the Neue Galerie New York, respectively—form parts of a much larger collection. My collection expanded exponentially from that first group of Miami hotels, branching out over the years to cover diverse interests, whether long-standing or relatively new, in topics as varied as art and design, advertising, vernacular photography, propaganda, architecture, war, social history, political cartoons, aviation, and ethnography, among many others. I could never choose a favorite card, or even group of cards. Different sections have resonated with me at different times and for different reasons (and still do). My extensive section of vernacular U.S. photographic cards, for example, evokes an innocent America, before this country was a global power. These photographs—really a form of folk art—depict small-town fairs, or smiling people perched on paper moons in studio portraits, or proud workingmen posing with the tools of their trade. They suggest to me the quiet before the storm

of the First World War. Other cards, depicting the Ku Klux Klan or anti-Semitic caricatures, reflect the darker sides of humanity. A more recent collection of ethnographic cards fascinate me by their vivid suggestion of a traditional world that gave way to the imperatives of colonialism. Other cards call to mind personal moments. A group of gas station cartoons from World War II, for example, brings me back to my childhood, when rationing was part of daily life.

It would be impossible for this book, which presents a selection of some 400 postcards, to convey the breadth and depth of the collection as a whole. Yet we spent countless hours carefully choosing the postcards for this publication, and for its companion exhibition at the MFA, in order to reflect the broad vision of the collection. First of all, an image had to grab the viewer. But then it had to invite closer reading, vividly suggesting both the immediate moment and the bigger sociohistorical picture.

At the core of the selections for this book is a beautiful group of postcards by European avant-garde artists that reveals the artfulness of the medium. Looking at the intricate designs of the Vienna Secession's *Ver Sacrum* postcards or the bold *japonisme* in a set by the Belgian artist Gisbert Combaz, I recall many exciting moments as I uncovered these treasures in antique shops on London's Portobello Road or in book kiosks along the Seine. As an early participant in what came to be a second postcard craze, I was fortunate to be able to bring together a group of the best artistic masterpieces; many of them are highly sought-after prizes for today's collectors. These cards formed the kernel of my collection. They helped me understand that this small format represented a uniquely modern artistic medium for the turn-of-the-century artist who wanted to experiment with subject and style and to participate in a craze that reached all corners of the globe.

The timely subjects and the artists' use of the medium to spread their experimental styles also aided me in understanding that the postcard was much more than a novel art form. It also carried new ideas across borders and transmitted what it meant to be a modern person living in a modern age. The rest of the cards reproduced here explore various aspects of life at the turn of the century. A group of postcards of Paris serves as a launching pad, presenting the City of Light as the epitome of everything new and exciting during the Postcard Age. At the time, Paris encapsulated all of the novel experiences of the epoch, from *plein-air* cafés and cabarets to world's fairs and new forms of transportation. These cards take me back to that moment when postcards were an integral aspect of the dynamic new century.

The selections that follow suggest connections between the most popular subjects and progressive styles of the Postcard Age. Some cards bring to life the excitement of urban diversions like skating rinks, public zoos, and amusement parks, which offered new opportunities for public interaction, and they recall the thrills that could be expected even from a walk down a city street. Others take us back to the glamorous era of express trains and the great transatlantic ocean liners—powerful machines that sliced through time and embodied the promise of adventure. Royals, political figures, and other celebrities, some long forgotten, whose activities were eagerly followed and discussed, make a vivid reappearance. Advertisements for commercial products (some obscure and others still in use today) display surprisingly contemporary wit and graphic ingenuity. Postcards that fed other crazes, like those for sports, bicycling, and fashion, complete the picture: not simply a nostalgic view of the past but a visual collage of the fast-paced early decades of the twentieth century, when these small images bombarded people from display racks or mailboxes and spoke the language of modernity. To understand this moment truly, I believe, we must recognize the postcard as one of its most ubiquitous and defining elements.

Over time, I have brought together cards from different periods, created for various events, and by countless artists into a carefully assembled collection. Each card speaks to the others in its group, and each group talks to the others. The collection is not merely an amassing of singular items, but rather a montage of objects that together say what each could not say on its own. I hope that this book, and its related exhibition, will offer the opportunity to explore the immediacy of the past.

In December 2002 I read Eugene Thaw's essay "The Art of Collecting" in *The New Criterion*. His opening lines, which sought to define what collecting means, resonated with me. Collecting is not, he wrote, about accumulating or investing. Rather, it is "acquiring objects that have some relation to each other and putting those objects into the kind of order that reflects the collector's response to them. Each true collection achieves a personality beyond and apart from the sum of the objects. This personality is definable and has a value in itself. It is lost if the collection is dispersed or mutilated."[3]

I have endeavored to form a collection that joins together various strands of history—art, graphic design, politics, and the forgotten aspects of daily life—and that brings to the fore the unique role the postcard medium played in that history. The postcard moves effortlessly between the public and the personal, allowing each of us today to make connections and explore historical interests in our own way, just as it did for those who experienced the original postcard craze. In deciding to pledge my collection to the MFA, I have been gratified that from the start the curators there have understood my vision of the postcard and what it means as a modern form of both art and communication.

In addition, my collaborators at the museum have understood the difficulties and responsibilities of preserving the spirit of the postcard and presenting it to the public. I am confident that I am entrusting my collection to a most capable, wise, and enthusiastic team of people who have joined me in succumbing to the postcard craze. I am particularly grateful to Malcolm Rogers, Ann and Graham Gund Director, and Katie Getchell, Deputy Director, for envisioning innovative ways in which the collection could contribute

LIE   Monta

to the MFA's objectives as an institution. Ben Weiss, the Leonard A. Lauder Curator of Visual Culture, quickly and keenly grasped the postcard's uniqueness and importance as a medium, as can be seen in his work on this publication and the related exhibition. I am elated that these cards will rejoin my Japanese collection, already at the MFA under the knowledgeable oversight of the museum's pioneer in postcards, Anne Nishimura Morse, William and Helen Pounds Senior Curator of Japanese Art. Christraud Geary, Teel Senior Curator of African and Oceanic Art, is a leader in the postcard field and shared her expertise with me as I built my African photographic collection, which has already entered the museum's collection. I have to thank many others on the MFA's extraordinary staff, including Virginia Durruty, whose exhibition design reflects both our collective enthusiasm for the postcard and the dynamics of the Postcard Age, and the talented publications team, editor Jennifer Snodgrass, book designer Susan Marsh, production manager Terry McAweeney, production coordinator Anna Barnet, and publisher Emiko Usui.

Over the years, I have counted on the expertise and camaraderie of many postcard colleagues and would like to acknowledge gratefully my longtime collaborator Detlef Hilmer, along with Robert Bogdan, George Gibbs, Dennis Goreham, Francis Gresse, Lee Jablin, Marc Lefebvre, Mary L. Martin, Anthony d'Offay, Don and Newly Preziosi, Francis Rottier, Douglas Wayne, and my old friend Joel Wayne. In the related world of the poster, the wisdom of Jack Rennert has been invaluable. I would also like to thank my own staff, including Anna Jozefacka, Luise Mahler, and Jocelyn Elliott, for their tireless research and organizational efforts in the preparation of this publication and exhibition. I owe a great debt of gratitude to Emily Braun for her unerring guidance over the many years that she has served as Curator of the Leonard A. and Evelyn H. Lauder Collection, and to Lynda Klich, Curator of the Leonard A. Lauder Postcard Collection, for sharing my passion for postcards and for her role in the organization of this book and exhibition.

In closing, I must thank my late wife, Evelyn Hausner Lauder (1936–2011), my partner and love for more than fifty-two years. She supported me in every step, and joined in sharing my special finds each time I arrived home with a new batch of postcards. She frequently laughed, as she did often, while claiming that I had a mistress—it was my postcard collection.

Evelyn, this exhibition and publication are dedicated to you and your unconditional love and support of all the insane things that I did. Your good humor and clear eye and patience with me helped bring this lifetime project to fruition.

1. "Per la storia delle cartoline postali illustrate," *Giornale della libreria, della tipografia, e delle arti ed industrie affini*, vol. 10 (Milan: Associazione Tipografico-Libraria Italiana, 1897), 413; Norman Alliston, "Pictorial Post-cards," *Chambers's Journal* 11 (Oct. 21, 1899): 745; and Naomi Schor, "*Cartes Postales*: Representing Paris 1900," *Critical Inquiry* 18 (Winter 1992): 212.
2. Leonard A. Lauder, "Collector's Preface," in Anne Nishimura Morse et al., *Art of the Japanese Postcard: The Leonard A. Lauder Collection at the Museum of Fine Arts, Boston*, exh. cat. (Boston: Museum of Fine Arts, 2004), 9–13, and "My Vienna Modern," in Elisabeth Schmuttermeier and Christian Witt-Dörring, eds., *Postcards of the Wiener Werkstätte: A Catalogue Raisonné; Selections from the Leonard A. Lauder Collection* (Ostfildern: Hatje Cantz Verlag, 2010), 11–15.
3. E. V. Thaw, "The Art of Collecting," *The New Criterion* 21, no. 4 (Dec. 2002): 13.

THE POSTCARD AGE

PARIS

From the top of the Eiffel Tower, 300 meters in altitude, I send my best kisses to my pretty Rosa, to my pretty Renée, and to my dear little Raphaël.

— V. MEYRET

It is August 2, 1889, and Monsieur V. Meyret sends a postcard from the top of the Eiffel Tower. He does not say why he is writing from 300 meters in the air, but he doesn't really have to.

In August 1889 the Eiffel Tower was the center of everyone's attention—in Paris and beyond. Not yet a year old, it was the trademark of the city's greatest spectacle, the sprawling Universal Exposition, which had risen like a dream on the dusty Champ de Mars, a former military parade ground on the south bank of the Seine. Whether he came from near or far, M. Meyret, like more than thirty million others, was eventually drawn to the fair. It offered dozens of buildings and hundreds of exhibits, with everything from a Javanese gamelan orchestra to gigantic steam engines and treasures of art. An ascent of the tower was the capstone of the whole experience.

The great exposition marked the hundredth anniversary of the French Revolution and was meant to highlight the great accomplishments of the modern state born of that convulsion. At the fair's center, the organizers wanted to "astonish the world with some grand achievement, the like of which had never been seen before."[1] They contracted with Gustave

Eiffel, who had already devised bridges of previously unimagined delicacy and grace, to construct a modern wonder. The elegant tower he delivered was the tallest man-made structure on Earth, nearly twice as high as its nearest rival—the great obelisk-shaped monument to George Washington, a key figure in that other late eighteenth-century revolution.

The towers could not have been more different. Whereas visitors to the top of the Washington Monument were confined to a bunker-like space as they strained to peer through tiny windows, Eiffel's tower was light and airy. Ascending it was like riding up on a balloon. You climbed into the elevator—something of a novelty itself—the grillwork gates closed, and the earth fell away. At a rate of just under ten kilometers an hour, a bit faster than a brisk walk, you floated higher than Notre Dame, higher than the dome of the Invalides, and past the birds, with the tower's great girders and beams gracefully crisscrossing beneath you. The people below became like ants, then almost disappeared altogether. It was a completely novel experience.

In keeping with that novelty, the tower did not dress itself in historical clothing, as so many grand buildings of the era did. Instead, it was aggressively up-to-date. Its bones were steel, a material associated with industrial wonders; its arteries were powerful hydraulic elevators; and the great electric light at the top, one of the most powerful yet devised, gazed out with the "transmuted energy of engines of 500

Du sommet de la tour Eiffel à 300 mètres d'altitude, j'envoie mes meilleurs baisers, à ma bonne Rosa, à Ma bonne Renée et à mon cher petit Raphaël—

Paris 2 8⁹ 1889

V. Meyret

4 Eiffel Tower, 1889

horsepower." Turning like a lighthouse beacon, the beam passed through a series of lenses—red, clear, blue—that broadcast France's *tricolore* across the city "from the loftiest flagstaff in the world."[2]

The fair's organizers made much of the tower's utility as an experiment in steel construction, as a platform for scientific observation, even as a lookout in times of war.[3] But like the exposition that spread out around it, the tower was first and foremost a tourist attraction. The trip to the top took three elevator rides, and each pause provided a chance to dally. The first platform, by far the largest, boasted no fewer than four restaurants, including an inexpensive Flemish *brasserie* and a French restaurant decorated in the style of Louis XIV, where the prices were "like the situation, high." Each restaurant boasted a balcony for dining *en plein air*, and at least one featured live entertainment every night.[4] The spaces around the restaurants were filled with newsstands, shops, and souvenir kiosks, creating a Parisian boulevard in miniature [6].

Having eaten your fill, or just paused for a drink, you took the elevator to the next stage. The second platform was much smaller than the first, but still held

"several shops, a Viennese bakery, and a newspaper office." The Paris daily *Le Figaro* had set up a press here, and each day published a miniature edition of the paper, at an altitude of 460 feet [7–8]. Higher still, a full five minutes by elevator, was the goal, at least for the public. (Above it were Eiffel's private apartment, a laboratory, and the gigantic electric beacon.) The elevator opened onto a mostly enclosed room, with windows and telescopes all around. In the middle was "a circle of desks . . . and accommodations for writing notes, post-cards, and telegrams to be posted and sent from the 'Top of the Eiffel Tower.'"[5] There, on August 2, for just a minute, we would have found M. Meyret, writing his postcard [4].

His note doesn't say much. It is a declaration that he has been to the top, a statement that he had done the new thing—that he was, in one small way at least, up-to-date. It is a safe bet that, having written his greeting and entrusted it to the mails, Meyret then spent a few minutes taking in the view. For though the tower was among the wonders of the world, the city below was the greater wonder still. Even guides to the exposition itself, such as a special edition of London's

9 (detail)

Pall Mall Gazette published for English visitors, admitted it: "There are many things to see in Paris, but the most important thing is to see Paris itself. Paris is more than any Exhibition. Exhibitions are all more or less modelled on the same pattern. Paris is unique."[6]

With one sweep of the eye, a visitor to the tower could take in what was, by universal agreement, the most remarkably modern place in the world. More than two millennia old, Paris had reinvented itself almost completely during the previous few decades. The government had cut long, straight boulevards through the city's tangle of medieval streets. New buildings and whole new districts had sprouted up around the old core. Gaslights had supplanted braziers and were in turn being replaced by bright new electric street lighting. A subway was in the works, and even the city's sewers had become a tourist attraction, offering visitors an experience so sanitary that "ladies need have no hesitation in taking part," according to Baedeker.[7]

The boulevards had helped speed a transformation of public life and leisure that began as early as the 1820s. Open to all, the new streets provided a welcoming environment for such novelties as grand cafés, where one could linger for hours, and huge department stores that offered *entrée libre*—"free entry"—the promise that a customer could browse unmolested by a shopkeeper. One American visitor was stunned at "the moving mass of promenaders on the pavements . . . so great that it often becomes necessary to stop and stand aside until there is an opportunity of moving on. Along the curb-stones are lines of chairs for rent, and the thousands of cafés are allowed to occupy about eight or ten feet along their front with their refreshment-tables, where the people sit and rest, and refresh themselves with coffee and ices."[8] The city offered theaters and restaurants and cabarets; the opera, the ballet, shopping beyond compare; the hint of political and sexual adventure; an avalanche of newspapers, journals, posters, and postcards; and, always, beautiful or at least interesting things and people to look at [9–12]. Paris was, as Mark Twain put it, full of citizens who were "so moustached, so affable, so fearfully and wonderfully Frenchy!"[9]

All of this is different now. The tower is still there, and the experience of rising up in the elevators is much the same. You can still mail a postcard, though from the bottom of the tower, not the top. The summit remains dizzyingly high, and Paris still stretches out below in all its elegant splendor. But the effect has changed completely. Going to the top of the Eiffel Tower is still a thrill ride, but it is also a historical exercise. Paris—resplendent, glittering Paris—no longer seems so modern. To look out over the city today is to see a monument to nineteenth-century urban planning rather than an exemplar of the new; to ascend the tower is to slip back a century.

But for Twain and Baedeker and the readers of the *Pall Mall Gazette*—and perhaps even for M. Meyret—the Paris of the end of the nineteenth century was the very symbol of modernity. In the decades around 1900 the city served as a showplace for novelty: new technologies, new artistic styles, new ways of living and being entertained, new manners and morals (both good and bad), and new ways of communicating—including postcards. By no means did Paris invent all the novelties of the age, but over and over it brought them into focus and then beamed them out again into the world.

It is hard to summon up that sense of novelty and possibility after the passage of more than a century. But this book and the exhibition it accompanies are, at least in part, an attempt to do so, using the postcard as a vehicle of time travel. Postcards, in their multiplicity, their immediacy, and their true democracy—even the most expensive originally cost but pennies to buy or post—provide a wonderful mirror of the broad concerns and obsessions of the age. To tease out some of those concerns, we have arranged the cards not by style or country but by themes: war, commerce, technology, the relationship between men and women. Such an approach presents a historical challenge. Big themes are susceptible to being painted with the broadest of brushes, and it is essential to keep in mind the tension between overarching historical developments and the particular, everyday experience of the past.

Postcards, because they were mass media, illuminate those big ideas and events. Yet they also have the power to bring the focus back down to individuals and their experiences. The personal messages they bear—a quick note from the top of the Eiffel Tower, for example—can open tiny but evocative historical windows into private life. Even when artists and advertisers and publishers used them to deliver messages to a mass audience, the cards delivered those messages to one person at a time. As images and ideas meant to be held in the hand—a very intimate exchange—postcards grant access to the texture of everyday life in a way few other sources do. They remind us, for example, that Paris was not just the magnificent view from the top of the Eiffel Tower. It was also smaller, more fleeting moments: one little girl smiling and pointing as she walks along the tower's platform, a particular butcher's display window, a moment of traffic congestion, a now forgotten celebrity.

Postcards survive in uncountable numbers. Perhaps because of that, they tempt us to look quickly. But if you slow down and look at them one by one, they provide unusually vivid access to the past. And the more you look, the more complicated the story they tell.   B.W.

1. Gaston Tissandier, *The Eiffel Tower: A Description of the Monument, Its Construction, Its Machinery, Its Object, and Its Utility; With an Autographic Letter of M. Gustave Eiffel* (London: Samson Low, Marston, Searle, and Rivington, 1889), 82.
2. "Paris and Its Exhibition," *Pall Mall Gazette Extra*, July 26, 1889, 36.
3. Tissandier, *The Eiffel Tower*, 83–84; Gustave Eiffel, *La Tour Eiffel en 1900* (Paris: Masson, 1902), 15–16.
4. "Paris and Its Exhibition," 39.
5. Thomas Ball, *My Threescore Years and Ten: An Autobiography* (Boston: Roberts Brothers, 1891), 357.
6. "Paris and Its Exhibition," 10.
7. Karl Baedeker, *Paris and Environs: With Routes from London to Paris and from Paris to the Rhine and Switzerland*, 8th rev. ed. (Leipzig: Karl Baedeker, 1884), 79.
8. Charles Carroll Fulton, *Europe Viewed through American Spectacles* (Philadelphia: J. B. Lippincott, 1874), 150.
9. Mark Twain, *The Innocents Abroad, or The New Pilgrim's Progress* (Hartford, Conn.: American Publishing Company, 1869), 113.

114. PARIS — Tour Eiffel. C. L. C

1009 PARIS. — La Tour Eiffel, Galerie extérieure du prem...

6

5
Eiffel Tower, before 1904

6
Eiffel Tower, first level, after 1903

5

7–8

Eiffel Tower, second level,
after 1903

7

8

9

9
Grand Café, after 1903

10
Dupont's Butcher Shop,
after 1903

11
Boulevard Montmartre,
after 1903

12
Rue Mouffetard,
after 1903

10

11

949 PARIS — Rue Mouffetard. — LL

12

13

Theater of the Guillaume boys,
Universal Exposition, 1900
ALBERT-ANDRÉ GUILLAUME

14

La Burgeatine liqueur,
about 1900
NOVER

13

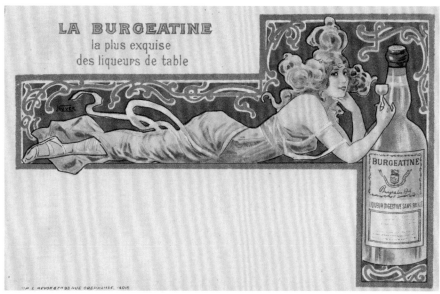

14

Un petit malentendu.

15

Les petits profits du souffleur.

16

15
A little misunderstanding
CARLOS BADY

16
The prompter's small perks
CARLOS BADY

THE CRAZE

[The postcard] takes possession of everyone, penetrates everywhere: the palaces of kings are as open to it as the humble cottage; it has loyalists in the city and in the village; all resistance is in vain.

— CHARLES SIMOND, "La carte postale," 1903

In the years around 1900, no English magazine had a firmer hold on its readers than London's *Strand*. From its very first issue in 1891, which "entered every omnibus, and took itself off in every departing train," it was a runaway success. *The Strand Magazine* was where Sherlock Holmes met his audience, where Queen Victoria published a drawing of her own children, and where a young Winston Churchill presented a thrilling account of his hunting trip through Britain's colonies in East Africa. The magazine's formula, a genial mix of light fiction, travel writing, gentle satire, and just a bit of politics, was in keeping with the founding editor's goal of providing the public with "cheap, healthful literature."[1]

In May 1903, tucked between a short story about the colorful lives of sailors and an article about cricket, readers found a short piece called "Some Puzzle-Picture Post-cards." The article, whose author signed himself simply "A Collector," introduced the *Strand*'s readers to a new sort of diversion: postcard puzzles, in which the picture was divided among several cards—charming and, at their best, baffling sets where the bodies of storks look like clouds, and

giraffes and hippopotami come in many parts. The *Strand*'s editors aimed to include at least one picture on every page, and this article came with an abundance of wonderful images. Front and center on the first page are photographs of three postcards that, when assembled, make a picture of a frog "seated in a somewhat stately manner in the middle of a country road" [20].[2]

The author admitted right up front that the frog puzzle was not very hard. Only the middle card was much of a mystery on its own. But the theme of the story is not the cards themselves so much as the author's experience of receiving them. He had not bought the cards himself, nor had they all come together in a package. Instead, a playful and rather wicked friend had been sending cards from a number of puzzles one by one, in no particular order, during a months-long trip to Germany. Every few days the postman would bring another installment, solving one problem or creating a new one. The result was a pleasurable torture, the delight of charming, maddening things coming drip by drip through the mails [21, 22]. As the cards arrived in their "disconnected profusion," the writer became obsessed, losing sleep and drawing attention to himself on the train "by pulling out of my pocket some wonderful specimens of postcard art, and muttering over them as if I were an incipient madman."[3]

He was not alone. The turn of the twentieth century saw a craze or *manie* or obsession for post-

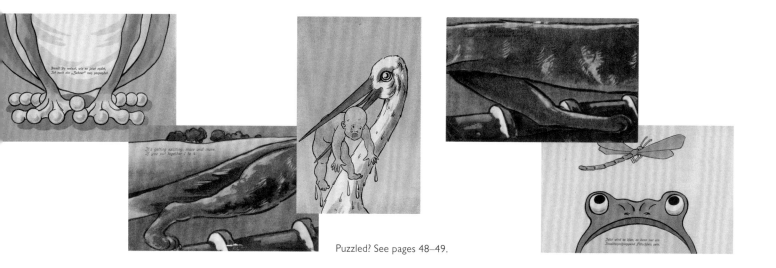

Puzzled? See pages 48–49.

cards—all words used at the time. The numbers are staggering. In 1903, for example, more than a billion cards passed through the German postal system.[4] In 1909 the British postal service sold 833 million stamps for postcards, nearly twenty for every man, woman, and child in the United Kingdom.[5] Whether they were tormented or delighted, obsessive or casual, those who sent and collected postcards relied on a smoothly functioning postal service. After all, what would happen to the puzzle if the stork's head went missing?

By 1903 the international postal system guaranteed the friend in Germany that a card dropped in a Munich postbox would find its way quickly and safely to a house in suburban London. That certainty was due to the work of the Universal Postal Union, based in Switzerland, which set the rules that governed the mail. Every few years, postal officials from around the globe met—in Bern or Lisbon or Washington, D.C.—to work through tricky questions like who was responsible for costs when mail from one country was shipped to another, or what size envelope required extra postage, or what size a postcard could be. The Union created an orderly structure that allowed letters, parcels, and postcards to be carried to every corner of the world predictably and efficiently. The rules had to be the same from country to country or

the intricate international machine that was the mail system would grind to a halt.[6]

That system was just one product of a broader movement toward internationalization that marked the second half of the nineteenth century. In the five decades between 1850 and 1900, European nations were knit together by adopting, among other things, standardized measurement (the metric system), identical railroad gauges, compatible electrical grids, and uniform time zones. It is one of the great ironies of the age that a time of surging and aggressive nationalism—a force that would ultimately rip the continent apart in the First World War—also saw unprecedented international cooperation. The mails were one key to that development. They smoothed the path for commerce and intellectual exchange and helped foster a broader sense that the cultures of Europe were entwined as never before.

Generally, the stories told about this age of globalization revolve around large economic and geopolitical forces—empire, colonialism, technology, and trusts. But the postcard craze shows it had more personal and domestic faces as well. At the turn of the century, the postcard was but a few decades old. Though it is difficult to think of something as familiar as a postcard being new and challenging, the cards were in fact a new communication technology. And like any new

technology, postcards were disruptive. As these small pieces of sturdy paper changed patterns of behavior and altered expectations about privacy and public morals, they prompted a great deal of debate.

The Austro-Hungarian post office issued the first prepaid postal cards—letters without envelopes—in 1869. Those first cards were very simple, with one side reserved for the message, the other for the address. They were an instant success. Customers sent them by the millions, earning the post office a tidy profit. In short order, almost every postal service in Europe, the Americas, and Asia followed suit, and nearly all racked up similar sales.[7] The cards filled a clear practical need. As a cheap and efficient way to send a note, postcards quickly came to embody the concept of the rapid message at a time when telephones were still rare. In an age when mail zipped through cities like Paris and New York via pneumatic tubes, and some urban homes received postal deliveries two or three times a day, one could jot down a line or two in the morning to arrange an afternoon meeting.[8]

But just as today's electronic means of communication have been seen as threats to the proper use of language and to social propriety, so, too, were postcards. For one thing, the short messages that fit on the cards could hardly convey the erudition of a traditional letter, a longtime sign of refinement. Some felt that the postcard's open nature promoted the circulation (and in effect endorsement) of potentially libelous statements.[9] The lack of an envelope also exposed one's personal affairs in an unprecedentedly public manner, not only to postal workers but also—perhaps more threateningly—to the servants who brought the mail to its final recipient. Some believed that sending an unsolicited postcard was an unmannerly violation of the recipient's privacy. The sheer volume of the new form of mail could also intimidate governments: in Italy, the popular author Jacopo Gelli, an early supporter of the postcard, noted that the cards "almost terrified" the Italian bureaucracy, which dragged its feet in adopting them.[10]

And there was the question of public morals. The very first postcards had been plain, but publishers and businesses soon recognized the opportunity to grace the fronts of cards with scenes of faraway places, advertisements for products, and all manner of greetings and cartoons. Not all the images were so innocuous, though, and while truly pornographic cards almost never went through the mails without an envelope, plenty of postcards played right up to the edge of being risqué. In 1901 the Italian printers' association appealed to the government to stave off the "invasion" of postcards that freely exposed "indecent" figures and so imperiled "public morality."[11] The French newspaper *Le Matin* called for a ban on vulgar postcards, since they disrupted the tranquility of the respectable home by making the recipient the laughingstock of the postman and servants.[12]

This uneasiness led to heated public debate. The writer Jules Claretie, a member of the Académie française, the august body that serves as a board of review for French grammar and vocabulary, demonstrated a widely shared ambivalence about the postcard. He acknowledged its power as a means of communication, yet noted with concern that "it has modified manners by revolutionizing the way we write." Yes, the postcard did away with the "torture" of letter writing—"a letter, *quelle fatigue!*"—and saved time. But he wondered whether the gain in convenience outweighed the loss of the exquisite art of epistolary correspondence, an especially French branch of literature that served as "one of the forces of our civilization." Claretie concluded that the postcard was perhaps the "biggest gift to human laziness." He equated it with another imported product that threatened an equally revered aspect of French culture: in offering a mere "slice of friendship" compared to a letter, the postcard was but "a beef bouillon cube of affection."[13]

Some prized the postcard for this very conciseness. The French composer Xavier Leroux noted that it offered a convenient excuse for laconic or indifferent communication, as opposed to a letter that demands "a bit of one's self."[14] The requisite terseness, combined with the postcard's connotation of speed, made the cards just as much a sign of the fast pace of contemporary life as other inventions of the day, such as the typewriter and the electric streetcar. As Frederick T. Corkett, of Great Britain's largest postcard publisher, Raphael Tuck & Sons, put it in a lecture to that country's esteemed Society of Arts: the postcard is "part and parcel of the busy, rushing, time-saving age we live in."[15]

Germany paved the way for the craze. The high quality of German cards attracted admiration and brought that country's printers a great deal of business, including contracts for cards intended for use in England, France, and the United States. Observers from other countries marveled at both the advanced nature of the German postcard industry and the country's astounding consumption of cards. During the first six months of 1898, Germans mailed over twelve million postcards; not even four years later, they were sending almost that number in a single week.[16] Not everyone was equally pleased by the cards' omnipresence. Chroniclers of the craze repeatedly noted the plight of the afflicted, buried under piles of cards and straining to keep pace with unending correspondence [23]. In 1900, a Viennese railway inspector and playwright wrote a bit of doggerel musing on how wonderful it would be if one could be all alone on a desert island with one's love: no fashion, no politics or news, and no one trying to be chic. A place with no post office—and no postcards! The poem was, of course, printed on a postcard.[17]

One target of satire was the tourists who spent their time in vacation spots seeking out the best postcards of local attractions rather than actually visiting the sites themselves. The Germans, who had succumbed to the postcard first, came in for particular mockery on this score, especially from the English. The humorist Jerome K. Jerome remarked that the typical German tourist did not even know where he had been until he returned home and examined the postcards he had sent to family and friends.[18] Returning from a Rhineland tour, the journalist George Robert Sims observed: "You enter the railway station, and everybody on the platform has a pencil in one hand and a postcard in the other. In the train it is the same thing. Your fellow travelers never speak. They have little piles of picture postcards on the seat beside them, and they write monotonously."[19] The pursuit of desirable cards could turn nasty. Jerome again: "A woman would pounce on a tray of cards, commence selecting, suddenly the tray would be snatched from her. She would burst into tears, and hit the person nearest to her with her umbrella. The cunning and the strong would secure the best cards. The weak and courteous [would] be left with pictures of post offices and railway stations."[20]

Many of these cards were thrown away after they had served their purpose. But not all, as the craze for buying and sending postcards was married to a craze for collecting them. Late nineteenth-century society was showered in a perpetual blizzard of little pieces of paper, and even very practical bits of ephemera became sought after. Photographic visiting cards, printed advertising cards, hatcheck stubs, tobacco cards, cigar bands, bookplates, postage stamps, and tram tickets—all had their collectors. The postcard eclipsed them all. It had always been possible to exchange collectibles, but with postcards the impulse to gather and arrange was married to the mail. With the payment of a few cents, centimes, or pfennig, cards could take themselves halfway around the world. Whole collections arrived through the mails. The onslaught of postcards wreaked havoc on postal systems; anecdotes about overburdened postal workers who left bags of cards undelivered abounded.[21] Yet millions upon millions of postcards were printed and never mailed. Instead, they were tucked into albums, unused and in mint condition. Collectors' albums, in models ranging from inexpensive to deluxe, became de rigueur in middle-class homes. The cleverly designed albums contained precut sheets with slits that allowed collectors to arrange cards to their best advantage [31, 34].

Collections most often focused on views of places near and far, or on a favorite topic, such as women or flowers. The director of the Comptoir Parisien, one of Paris's biggest postcard publishers, filled an album with cards depicting the tombs of famous French writers, poets, musicians, artists, and scientists. It was not a macabre topic, he insisted, but rather, a way for a child to learn that was "a thousand times more interesting" than conventional lessons.[22] Charles Simond, a chronicler of turn-of-the-century Paris, paid the postcard craze the ultimate compliment, when he observed that postcard collectors

31 (detail)

had come to rival in their passion collectors of that longstanding object of pursuit—the postage stamp.[23]

Artists sensed a market. Some, like the German painter Emil Nolde, found the postcard to be a lucrative sideline to their work in the so-called high arts. Around 1896, as a young unknown, he created a series of cards under his original surname of Hansen [17]. The artist Paula Modersohn-Becker wrote to her sister Milly about the cards with admiration, though perhaps not quite with respect: "He got the clever idea, when he was in Switzerland, of picture postcards with views of the Alps, the Jungfrau [Young Woman], Mönch [Monk], Eiger [Ogre], and so forth, each one with an expressive face. . . . Being the sly little peasant he is, he published them himself and in one week he earned ten thousand marks. Now his banner is emblazoned with the sign of True Art and he has serious aspirations."[24] Other artists sus-

17 Old Saint Gotthard, 1897 EMIL HANSEN (EMIL NOLDE)

18 The favorite, 1900 RAPHAEL KIRCHNER

tained entire careers with the postcard. The Austrian Raphael Kirchner was perhaps the most prolific, creating more than 125 series of postcards featuring coquettish women (all modeled on his wife, Nina) that were published throughout the world between 1898 and 1917. Soldiers hung Kirchner's cards in the trenches during World War I, earning him a reputation as the father of the pinup [18].

Postcards could even serve as artistic manifestos. In the 1890s, groups of young artists were "seceding" from official schools and art academies all over Europe, forming groups that set out to reform the arts under the banner of the avant-garde. Using postcards to advertise the new styles was especially popular in Germany and Austria: collectives and publishers from Dresden to Karlsruhe to Vienna issued extensive sets of cards that explored the new forms of Jugendstil (Young Style), as art nouveau is called in German. These artists helped turn the postcard into an art form discussed in leading art journals, such as London's *Studio International*, Berlin's *Pan*, Brussels's *L'art moderne*, and Milan's *Emporium*.

In their journey to artistic acceptance, postcards followed a road first traveled by the advertising poster, another object of public infatuation during the 1890s. Countless famous posters, including those of Jules Chéret, the medium's founding father, took on a second life on postcards. Many noted the family resemblance, though not everyone approved. Some ranked postcards as inferior to their larger cousins, calling them "meretricious miniature posters" or disparaging the cards because their artists mostly left them unsigned.[25] On a more positive note, others pointed out that the postcard's small size and transportability made it an *affiche roulante*, or "poster on wheels."[26] Indeed, as the Toronto journal *Bookseller and Stationer* reported in 1899, the large size of posters made it so difficult to manage a collection that "the post card has quite knocked out the poster."[27]

Soon, enthusiasts began organizing international exhibitions dedicated to the postcard. The first took place in Leipzig, a major center of postcard publishing, in May 1898, and the idea spread quickly. The next two years saw shows in Monaco, Florence, Nice, Geneva, Ostend, Venice, Budapest, and Warsaw. In a review of the First International Illustrated Postcard Exhibition, held at Venice's Palazzo della Zecca in August 1899, Aldo Maggioni noted that if, just a few years before, one had suggested an exhibition made up entirely of postcards, he would have "smiled in disbelief." But now this exhibition confirmed that the public had undergone a "healthy awakening to a sense of design," and wanted quotidian objects to "caress or tickle the eye."[28]

Such shows took in the whole postcard industry: in addition to displaying the new miniature masterpieces created by the best illustrators, they dedicated space to journals, clubs, publishers, suppliers of albums, and, of course, collectors. The Venice exhibition, for example, displayed albums assembled by some of the most advanced postcard aficionados. A Signore Besso from Rome brought fourteen albums, which housed his collection of six thousand cards. The organizers proudly showcased the collection of an Italian aristocrat, the Marchesa Denti di Piraino, but one journal noted that a Miss Antonini's nine thousand cards made the biggest impression.[29]

Enthusiasts in places that were relative latecomers to the postcard clamored for a craze of their own, citing not only the economic benefits, but also a desire

that their countries might join other so-called civilized nations in this cultural pursuit. To make his case to the British public, the popular writer Norman Alliston let his readers in on a secret: Queen Victoria had taken such interest in the postcard that she had recently engaged "a royal relative to form a collection on her behalf."[30] This hint that postcard collecting was a refined pastime may have helped counter the postcard's supposed vulgarity.

The single most important factor in advancing the craze may have been the postcard's ubiquity at world's fairs. These enormous and expensive expositions were quintessential spectacles of the late nineteenth and early twentieth centuries, through which countries vied to demonstrate their national superiority. The organizers of each fair sought to surpass the previous ones, creating ever grander venues filled with ephemeral architectural wonders, illuminated fountains, and manmade lagoons and waterfalls. Ever since London had dazzled the world with the great iron-and-glass Crystal Palace in 1851, it seemed that each fair needed some signature technological marvel. In Paris in 1889 it was Gustave Eiffel's tower; in 1893, visitors to Chicago were captivated by George W. Ferris's giant wheel.

These temporary cities offered ideal sites for competitive displays of imperial reach and power. This was the age of European colonialism, and many fairs featured reconstructions of African, Asian, or Polynesian villages, inhabited by native peoples who lived under public scrutiny for months on end. The pavilions for the nations that sent exhibits often took the form of picturesque buildings meant to capture the essence of each country: half-timbered houses for England or pagodas for Japan [38]. Colorful spectacles like the Wild West shows starring Buffalo Bill and Annie Oakley that delighted Parisian crowds in 1889 helped cement perceptions of the United States as a land of freedom, adventure, and enticing lawlessness. Almost always, though, the largest buildings were those dedicated to machines. Nations used the fairs to showcase their technological ingenuity

and scientific genius. And because the expositions were largely supported by businesses, they served as launching pads for new products and inventions—everything from Cracker Jack and ice cream cones to electricity, zippers, and escalators.

The huge numbers of visitors generated a vast market for souvenirs and memorabilia. Fairs produced all manner of official trinkets such as spoons, coins, and toys that visitors carried home as proof of their firsthand experience of the great event.[31] Illustrated postcards were a decisively modern product that offered an up-to-date way to communicate the excitement and glamour of the fairs. Postcards could be produced quickly and in abundance, so they provided seemingly limitless opportunities for publicity. Almost every visitor could afford to buy postcards, and the cards greatly expanded the fair's audience as they were sent throughout the world. Official cards allowed organizers to reinforce the fair's branding or signal element.[32]

While picture postcards delighted fairgoers at the World's Columbian Exposition in Chicago in 1893, they took Paris's exposition of 1900 by storm. Numerous series offered scenes of the fair's distinctive structures, framed by different designs and marked with official logos. Cards featured panoramic or bird's-eye views of the grounds, or included images of individual areas, thoroughfares, and monuments. These cards both advanced the fair's nationalistic message and advertised products peddled by the fair's backers, such as Suchard chocolate [43]. The plethora of cards meant that even those who could not afford the new portable cameras that were all the rage in 1900 could still bring home images of their favorite places. Even entrance tickets to venues were attached to postcards and sold in booklet form [40–42].

The publishers who produced cards for the Paris exhibition did everything possible to encourage their consumption, helping shape the postcard industry for years to come. They sought to produce innovative or novel cards that would both entice established collectors and attract new buyers. Serial production was

an especially effective spur—"Collect them all!"—so publishers issued multiple, competing series, with different sorts and styles of views. The publishers also sought to tempt collectors with new sorts of products. One novelty from the 1900 fair that became a perennial favorite was the hold-to-light card. These cards are made from layered and cut papers, some opaque and some transparent. When placed in front of a light source, the cards either created the illusion of natural light or made the extravagant displays of electric lighting at the fair come to life. Such cards were a "must have" for the collector and a means to convey the wonder of the exposition to those not lucky enough to see it for themselves [39].

After the 1900 exposition, postcards were everywhere. Production increased exponentially during the first decade of the twentieth century, and observers around the world proclaimed proudly (or fearfully!) that their countries were finally caught up in the same craze as Germany. In 1902, the British innovation of the divided postcard back gave publishers an opportunity to come up with an even greater variety of cards to keep collectors in the chase. The first generation of postcards had allocated one entire side to the recipient's address. The image on the front had to share space with any message the sender added. Publishers and artists used different means to provide blank space for the message within the image itself. As illustrations became increasingly important to postcard collectors, some artists and publishers began designing cards that left no room for messages at all. In 1904, the French magazine Le Figaro illustré noted the phenomenon in a special issue devoted entirely to the postcard: "The illustration has become more and more invasive. At first timid in the corner of the card, it then occupied a more important place. One could write thirty words, then only ten. Next one was left with just a corner for a date and a signature, and now there's no room left to write."[33] The invention of the divided back solved the problem. The simple idea of printing a line down the center of the back allowed one side of the card to contain both message and address. Following Britain's lead, France adopted the new format in 1904 and led the charge for acceptance of what was then called the "international recto." Most countries were using the divided back by the time the United States finally implemented it on March 1, 1907.

The desire for international uniformity was partly driven by the demands of collectors, whose networks had begun to crisscross the world. Locally, they formed associations that met regularly to exchange cards and discuss the latest innovations [24]. Some groups also published postcard-collecting journals. These magazines tracked the figures associated with postcard consumption and hosted animated debates about the minutiae of postal regulations, rates, and tariffs. Contributors advocated cheaper postage to encourage their pastime, issuing manifesto-like proclamations cautioning against the readiness to "render unto Caesar" in the form of disproportionately high postage rates for postcards and calling on collectors everywhere to "claim the rights to which they are equally entitled."[34]

These journals encouraged communication from readers by organizing contests, including trivia quizzes and competitions for the best amateur postcard submitted by a subscriber. They even sponsored postal races, in which cards were mailed to the journal headquarters on the same day from zones throughout the world, with awards going to the sender whose card arrived first. Prizes were paid, of course, in postcards. Collectors' societies and their journals were keenly aware of the postcard's larger significance. As early as 1906, one journal called for the establishment of a national postcard museum in France, urging the government to preserve the millions of images that recorded the early twentieth century in unprecedented detail—a "goldmine for future generations." As the author added, somewhat wistfully: "Imagine if ancient Greece or Rome had possessed them!"[35]

But the centerpieces, and perhaps raisons d'etre, of such journals were the listings by collectors who sought partners for postcard exchanges. Reading much like personal ads, these announcements listed a collector's specific desires or indicated what he or she could provide in return. Luis F. Miranda, in Guayaquil, Ecuador, promised lovely views of his city in exchange for the same of yours. "Stecchi," an infantry captain hailing from Italy's Piedmont, would send complete series of cards from Italy. Walter H. Beddel, of Wellington, New Zealand, sought out any collector who wished to exchange cards of theater actors and actresses, while in Algeria, Mlle. Renée Boucher requested cards that depicted national types and costumes. Potential trading partners listed the languages in which they could correspond (the experimental universal language of Esperanto found a dedicated audience among postcard collectors). Some dictated exactly where to place the stamp on the cards, while many declared that "careless correspondents need not respond."[36]

The most requested type by far was the view card. During the first decade of the twentieth century, there was hardly a village in the world that was not the subject of a set of postcards featuring its best-known sites or most picturesque corners. View cards probably constituted around 90 percent of all postcards, and collecting such mass-manufactured images marked one as an up-to-date global citizen. Postcards connected their user to the wider world, whether near or far, familiar or exotic. The German Jewish polymath and philosopher of the modern world Walter Benjamin vividly remembered the effects postcard views had on him. A hold-to-light card of the Halle Gate in Berlin transformed the spot, fixing it indelibly in his memory as being lit by "the very same glow that came from the full moon up in the sky."[37]

Publishers continued to come up with fuel for the craze. They issued cards depicting an expansive array of subjects, from cats and dogs to soldiers and fashionable women, from humble local types to celebrities and royalty [19]. They encouraged artists, both well-known professionals and amateurs, to develop signature styles and novel ways of depicting every imaginable subject. Always, the goal was to produce

19 University of
Pennsylvania, 1907
F. EARL CHRISTY

new must-have variations on a theme. They issued cards for every holiday and cards that commented on the latest news.

Postcard producers also found ways to enhance the standard combination of ink and paper, adding glitter, embossing, and metallic inks. "Mechanical" cards boasted spinning color wheels or moving parts, and other cards were printed on silk, leather, or thin slices of wood. One great success was do-it-yourself cards that allowed a customer to take photographs with special Kodak film that could print directly onto postcard stock. Some postcard associations and journals offered to produce small print runs of cards on special order, and portrait studios joined in, printing their works on postcards that a sitter could buy in multiples and send to family and friends [47–48]. One enterprising publisher even invented a "postal phonograph" called the Sonorine. The sender recorded a voice message in a coin-operated booth that spat out a postcard containing a phonographic record. The message could then be played by the recipient, provided that the sender had also arranged for the delivery of a special small-sized phonograph, available of course at minimal cost.[38]

Such a craze could not last forever. As early as 1908, the *New York Times* reported on a somber meeting of German manufacturers, who concluded that a slump in the American market was causing their business to go "from bad to worse."[39] Yet other accounts continued to marvel at the tens of billions of postcards being produced, sold, and mailed annually. The advent of World War I began the industry's decline as it faced supply shortages, disrupted production, destroyed factories, as well as broken relations between Germany, the top supplier, and many of the countries that created the demand. Even so, publishers still produced substantial quantities of postcards throughout the 1920s and 1930s. Postcards went on to become important tools of state propaganda in Fascist Italy, Nazi Germany, Japan, and the Soviet Union. But the mania had passed, and the postcard was supplanted as the symbol of speed and modernity by other means of communication, such as the telephone and radio.

By the 1930s, postcards from the first decades of the century were already becoming objects of nostalgia. A new generation of collectors emerged, who sought vintage cards from the first craze. As sources of imagery and emblems of a bygone era, these postcards attracted artists and writers, including the Surrealists, who established their own postcard-trading network. As the poet Paul Eluard noted in an article about "the most beautiful postcards" published in the Surrealist journal *Minotaure* in 1933 that included illustrations of the pages of his own albums: postcards were more than mass culture, they were the "small change" left over from art that sometimes contained "ideas of gold."[40]

During the postcard's heyday, writers struggled to enumerate and categorize the craze. They almost uniformly described postcard collecting as an addiction, with collectors called fanatics, or deemed obsessed, as if the postcard induced some kind of inevitable madness. In 1904, Claretie had suggested that collectors were worthy of examination by Dr. Jean-Martin Charcot, the French scientist who pioneered the study of neuroses.[41] Indeed, in almost every language, the word used to describe the phenomenon classed it as a mania, an "-itis," an addiction, a disease, fever, ague, pathogen, infection, pest, or virus. Once the bug bit you, one writer observed, it "paralyze[d] the reasoning facilities."[42] "It takes a strong man to resist the practice," the British cartoonist Phil May observed in 1906.[43] Today it is probably impossible to conjure what Simond almost helplessly called this "idiotic battle of confetti." But, as he also noted, at the turn of the century the postcard was inescapable.[44]   B.W., L.K.

1. George Newnes, "Introduction," *The Strand Magazine* 1, no. 1 (January 1891): 3.
2. [A Collector], "Some Puzzle-Picture Post-cards," *The Strand Magazine* 25 (May 1903): 569–72.
3. Ibid., 572, 569.
4. Frederic T. Corkett, "The Production and Collection of the Pictorial Postcard," *Journal of the Society of Arts* 54 (April 27, 1906): 625.
5. Howard Woody, "International Postcards: Their History, Production, and Distribution (circa 1895 to 1915)," in *Delivering Views: Distant Cultures in Early Postcards*, ed. Christraud M. Geary and Virginia-Lee Webb (Washington, D.C.: Smithsonian Institution Press, 1998), 42; *www.parliament.uk/documents/commons/lib/research/rp99/rp99-111.pdf* (accessed 9/15/2011).
6. George A. Codding, Jr., *The International Postal Union: Coordinator of the International Mails* (New York: New York University Press, 1964), 25–47.
7. Martin Willoughby, *A History of Postcards: A Pictorial Record from the Turn of the Century to the Present Day* (London: Studio Editions, 1993), 30–32.
8. Molly Wright Steenson, "Interfacing with the Subterranean," *Cabinet* 41 (2011): 82–86.
9. "Inventor of the Postcard Dies," *New York Times*, August 3, 1902.
10. Jacopo Gelli, "Le cartoline illustrate e le cartoline Liebig," in *Almanacco Italiano: Piccola enciclopedia popolare della vita pratica e annuario diplomatico amministrativo e statistico, Anno V., 1900* (Florence: H. Bemporad e figlio, 1899), 484.
11. *La rassegna nazionale*, year 23, vol. 120 (July 16, 1901): 394.
12. F.S., "Cartes postales injurieuses," reprinted from *Le Matin*, in *Le collectionneur* 1, no. 7 (November 10, 1905): 2.
13. Jules Claretie, *La vie à Paris, 1904* (Paris: Bibliothèque-Charpentier, 1905), 101–4.
14. Xavier Leroux, letter published in *Le Figaro: Numero spécial: La carte postale illustrée* 175 (October 1904).
15. Corkett, "The Production and Collection of the Pictorial Postcard," 622–33.
16. H.W.S., "Studio Talk," *Studio International: An Illustrated Magazine of Fine and Applied Art* 14 (1898): 287–89; Frank L. Emanuel, "Pictorial Postcards. A General Survey," *The Magazine of Art*, n.s. 1 (1903): 88, citing the *Pall Mall Gazette*, November 1, 1902.
17. C. Karlweis, *Wien, das bist du! Kleine Erzählungen aus dem Nachlasse*, ed. Hermann Bahr and Vincenz Chiavacci (Stuttgart: A. Bonz, 1903); Johannes Horowitz, "What Interests Vienna," *New York Times*, January 7, 1900, 21.
18. Jerome Klapka Jerome, *The Angel and the Author—And Others* (London: Hurst and Blackett, 1908), 70.
19. G. R. Sims in *The Referee* (1900), cited in Richard Carline, *Pictures in the Post: The Story of the Picture Postcard and Its Place in the History of Popular Art* (Philadelphia: Deltiologists of America, 1972), 64.
20. Jerome, *Angel and the Author*, 72.
21. John Walker Harrington, "Postal Carditis and Allied Manias," *American Illustrated Magazine* 61 (March 1906): 566.

22. Rousell, "Le crise," *Le collectionneur universelle: Revue mensuelle carto-philatélique et littéraire* 3 (July 10, 1907): 83.

23. Charles Simond, "La carte postale," in *Paris de 1800 à 1900: Les centennales parisiennes; panorama de la vie de Paris à travers le XIXe siècle* (Paris: Plon-Nourrit, 1903), 150.

24. Paula Modersohn-Becker to Milly Becker, May 27, 1900, in *Paula Modersohn-Becker: The Letters and Journals*, ed. Günther Busch and Liselotte von Reinken, trans. and ed. Arthur S. Wensigner and Carole Clew Hoey (Evanston, Ill.: Northwestern University Press, 1998), 190; Emil Nolde, *Die Bergpostkarten*, ed. Magdalena M. Moeller (Munich: Hirmer, 2006).

25. Norman Alliston, "Pictorial Post-cards," *Chambers's Journal* 11 (October 21, 1899): 746; Simond, "La carte postale," 150.

26. M. R. Berga, "Les cartes postales illustrées," in *Congrès bibliographique international tenu à Paris du 13 au 16 avril 1898, Compte rendu des travaux* (Paris: Société Bibliographique, 1900), 2:129.

27. "Stationery Novelties in Europe: From Paris and Berlin Correspondence," *Bookseller and Stationer* 25, no. 10 (October 1899): 18.

28. Aldo Maggioni, "La I.ª esposizione internazionale di cartoline postali illustrate a Venezia: Note ed appunti," *Emporium* 10 (1899): 310–11.

29. Gelli, "Le cartoline illustrate e le cartoline Liebig," 490.

30. Alliston, "Pictorial Post-cards," 748.

31. James Gilbert, "World's Fairs as Historical Events," and Jon B. Zachman, "The Legacy and Meaning of World's Fair Souvenirs," in *Fair Representations: World's Fairs and the Modern World*, ed. Robert W. Rydell and Nancy Gwinn (Amsterdam: VU University Press, 1994), 23–24, 199–217.

32. Robert W. Rydell, "Souvenirs of Imperialism: World's Fair Postcards," in *Delivering Views*, 53–54.

33. *Le Figaro: Numero spécial: La carte postale illustrée* 175 (October 1904).

34. Charles de Straits, "Causerie," *Le collectionneur* 1, no. 2 (June 10, 1905): 4.

35. "Un musée national de la carte postale," *Carte postale revue* 1 (December 1906).

36. These examples were taken from issues of *Le collectionneur*; most postcard journals included similar sections.

37. Walter Benjamin, *The Arcades Project*, trans. Howard Eiland and Kevin McLaughlin (Cambridge, Mass.: Harvard University Press, 1999), 104.

38. *Le collectionneur* 8 (December 10, 1905): 3.

39. "Postcard Craze Is Dying," *New York Times*, December 27, 1908, C2.

40. Paul Eluard, "Les plus belles cartes postales," *Minotaure* 3–4 (December 1933): 87.

41. Claretie, *La vie à Paris,* 101–2.

42. Harrington, "Postal Carditis and Allied Manias," 562–67.

43. "Humour by Post, Illustrated Chiefly by Drawings from Phil May," *The Strand Magazine* 32 (September 1906): 180–85.

44. Simond, "La carte postale," 150.

20

Frog puzzle, about 1900

21

Cat puzzle, about 1900

22

Stork puzzle, about 1900

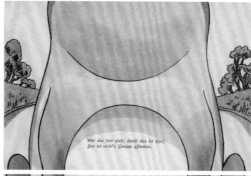
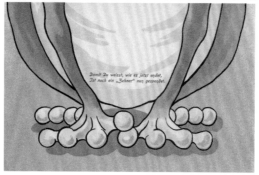

20

21

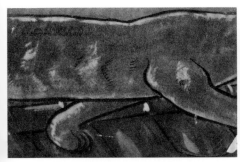

23

24

23

Postcard mania, about 1905

VAN DOCK (VINCENZO NASI)

24

Membership card, Carto-Philatélique Club, about 1904

ORENS DENIZARD

25
Postcard peddlers, Marseille,
about 1910

26
Enthusiasts and collectors,
about 1900

25

26

27

The postcard maintains friendship,
about 1904

28

Postcard tourists in Brussels,
about 1900

27

28

29

29
Advertising without competition, about 1905

30
The postcard, about 1900

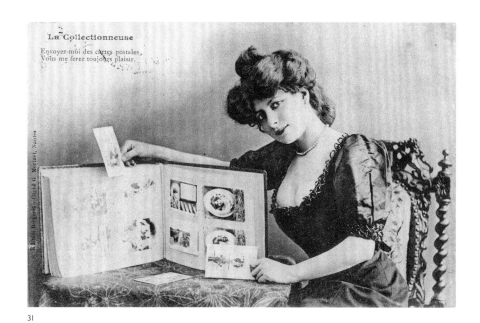

31

The collector, about 1909

GEORGES MORINET

32

Poster for Russian Red Cross
postcards, 1904

LÉON BAKST

THE CRAZE

33

34

33

Poster for exhibition of Christmas and
New Year's cards, Vienna, after 1898

T. H. OR H. T. BAUER

34

Poster for postcard exhibition, Paris,
about 1900

WILLIAM-ADOLPHE LAMBRECHT

35

36

37

38

39

40

41

42

40
Postcard-ticket to the Grand Cambodian
Theater, 1899

41
Postcard-ticket to the Naval Combat,
1899

42
Postcard-ticket book, 1899
G. GUIDI

43
Celestial Globe

43

44–46

College girls and boys, 1907

F. EARL CHRISTY

44

45

46

47

48

47

Woman on a paper moon, about 1910

S. M. JOHN

48

Man on a paper moon, about 1910

STYLE

These pieces of cardboard, pursued by postcard lovers and maniacs, sell for higher prices today than a Corot or Jules Dupré did in the past.

— JULES CLARETIE, *La vie à Paris*, 1904

Europe's *belle époque*, romanticized now as an age of urban diversions, flowing champagne, new technologies, and high fashion, would be difficult to conjure without the backdrop of art nouveau. The style's swirling lines and decorative patterns represented up-to-date culture and luxury as much as did the newfangled automobile or latest feathered hat. Architects such as Hector Guimard, Victor Horta, and Antoni Gaudí transformed cities with impossibly sinuous façades, richly patterned mosaics, and ironwork in intricate arabesques. Women wore dresses made from textiles tangled with printed scrolls and sported jewelry enlivened by webs of tendrils. Art nouveau styling could be found on silver, glassware, and ceramics in department stores like Printemps in Paris or Liberty of London, and even decorated restaurant menus, water fountains, and street signs.

In Europe and beyond, artists used this new visual language to manifest the excitement of a world undergoing transformation. August Endell, a German architect and designer, considered these new art forms to be a result of a "vehement yearning for a new style" that would help people see the world anew; its complex lines revealed "an immensely rich new world, full of totally new experience."[1] Art nouveau offered a way to remake daily life, as collaborations in fine art, graphic art, textile design, and furniture production transformed living spaces. The style's leading practitioners, such as the Belgian architect and designer Henry van de Velde, argued passionately for the joining of progressive design with industrial production as a way to eliminate hierarchical divisions between the applied and fine arts, thereby eliding class divisions and spurring social change.[2] In this proposed synthesis of the arts, the artist became a reformer, able to turn even the most humble object into a thing of beauty.

The zeal for updated forms did not result in a unified international style. Instead, artists who wanted to break from well-established academic rules or traditions banded together to create new styles—whether emphasizing curving linearity or dense geometric patterning—that responded to national concerns as much as to aesthetic priorities. The umbrella term for the style was invented by Siegfried Bing, a German entrepreneur who in December 1895 opened a decorative art shop in Paris named L'Art Nouveau. Also known more generally as "the modern style," its local variants included Secession style in Austria, Jugendstil in Germany, the Glasgow Style in Scotland, *Stile Liberty* in Italy (after the London store), and *modernismo* in Spain. All of these artistic movements shared a desire to break free from academic constraints through the inventive abstraction of form.

The push for progressive design styles developed

at the same time as the postcard craze. Like post-cards, art nouveau made a big splash at the 1900 Universal Exposition in Paris, where several national and commercial pavilions promoted it—famously those of Bing and the major French department stores Le Louvre, Le Bon Marché, and Printemps. Opponents viewed the new style, especially its commercialism, as artistic anarchy infiltrating the so-called high arts. Those who objected to the rapid spread of art nouveau felt that it offended good taste and challenged longstanding aesthetic values—much like the humble, democratic, and inexpensive postcard.[3]

Art nouveau and the postcard also shared supporters. Magazines that promoted the new visual styles, such as *L'art moderne* in Brussels and *The International Studio* in London and New York, featured articles on the postcard as a new art form. These supporters understood the postcard as one medium that fostered the democratization of the arts desired by art nouveau's proponents. In conjunction with this aim, schools of applied arts trained artists in both traditional media and so-called crafts—from painting and sculpture to furniture making and textile weaving—as well as the graphic arts. Run by progressive artists or affiliated with dissident groups, these associations often employed the postcard to advance their new art forms.

The Munich journals that were the foremost promoters of new styles in graphic arts—*Die Jugend* (Youth), known for fantastical imagery steeped in folk traditions, and *Simplicissimus*, which focused on social satire—published postcard series to disseminate the innovative illustrations that appeared on their covers. One of the earliest and most well-known sets of artists' postcards came from the Vienna Secession, which issued a series of twelve on the occasion of its first exhibition in 1898 to promote the group's progressive design aesthetic as well as its new avant-garde journal *Ver Sacrum* (Sacred Spring). Many of these cards combine the designs of two or three artists, such as Josef Hoffmann and Koloman Moser, resulting in densely symbolic depictions of figures in natu-

49 Postcard pavilion, Darmstadt colony, 1901
HANS CHRISTIANSEN

ral settings [54–55]. The alternating areas of deep, brilliant colors and shimmering gold emphasize flattened forms and linearity, lending the cards a sense of geometrical structure. While the artists make a nod toward the need for blank message space, their experiments with text, image, and decoration push the limits of postcard design much as they were challenging artistic traditions of all sorts.[4]

The German artist Hans Christiansen similarly explored the integration of image and message space. In his woman-flower designs, Christiansen creates a seamless dialogue between the outlines of the flowing hair and impossibly puffy flowers, and the surrounding white space [56–57]. He made these cards for the Darmstadt Künstlerkolonie, an artists' colony formed in 1899 to promote the applied arts. Like the colony's other members, Christiansen lived in a home especially designed for him, by the architect Joseph Olbrich; he created the cards to encourage visits to his house by those walking the colony grounds during exhibitions. Although the woman-flower was a common motif in art nouveau, Christiansen's version became something of a personal trademark. The same motif that appears on the postcard also adorned an exterior painting and a tapestry for his Darmstadt home, which was known as the Villa in Roses.[5]

Christiansen's series was part of a larger postcard publicity campaign by the Darmstadt colony, which sold cards at its first exhibition, "A Document of German Art," held in 1901, and at later ones even constructed special postcard pavilions on its grounds. The colony published several series, both illustrated and photographic, depicting the distinctive architecture—white stucco buildings with rounded edges, asymmetrical façades with colored accents in tile and stained glass, and traditional gabled roofs—of the houses and other structures built on its Mathildenhöhe estate, designed mostly by Olbrich [49]. The postcard series offered an efficient platform for artists' groups such as the Darmstadt colony to proclaim their allegiances, to promote exhibitions, products, and publications, and to help support themselves financially.

Many artists also welcomed the postcard as an exciting new artistic medium for experimenting with new techniques of color lithography that allowed for ever brighter and more varied hues. From the start, artist's postcards, as they were known, were considered to be a cut above the typical postcard produced for mass consumption. A writer in *The International Studio* remarked as early as 1898 that postcards had already been "raised from a trade to an art" by designers and printers in Germany and Belgium. A year later, the same magazine recommended that a series of cards of landscapes produced by the Karlsruhe Künstlerbund (artists' association) in 1897 "should be secured by all those who are interested in the modern development of lithographic art in Germany."[6] Rather than looking down on artists who worked in this popular medium, these critics perceived the postcard as a sign of the artistic times and an acceptable, even savvy, move by the forward-thinking artist.

At the first postcard exhibition, held in Leipzig in May 1898, more than ten thousand series of postcards were shown. Astonished at the numbers, the critic for the French magazine *L'art moderne* confirmed that the best artists were now "putting their brushes at the disposal" of postcard publishers, as they had done earlier with posters.[7] *Emporium* magazine published an extensively illustrated review of the August 1899 show at the Palazzo della Zecca in Venice, written by Aldo Maggioni. The critic suggested that the postcard had already distinguished itself from the poster, which was only concerned with quickly grabbing the viewer's attention: the postcard, which was more personal, also captured the viewer's mind, giving artists the opportunity to explore "careful and often bizarre choices of color, with clearly outlined figures, marked by a light or dark line, by strong contrasts of light and shade, decorated with friezes daring to strike the eye with their particular novel aspects."[8] Luigi Bompard's "Photography" postcards embody some of Maggioni's ideas. In a series of six cards, the artist uses eerie, disembodied female heads to represent different elements of the photographic process, including the lens, the negative, and the print [58–61]. One critic at the time dubbed the series "weird," a description intended to compliment its artistic audacity.[9]

Maggioni also argued that postcards responded more effectively than media such as photographs, watercolors, and small-scale paintings to the vital sense of design that now infused everyday life, thanks to the efforts of art nouveau's proponents. Postcards were on view at the Prima Esposizione d'Arte Decorativa Moderna, the first exhibition to showcase art nouveau's extensive reach and international stylistic development. Mounted in Turin's Valentino Park in

50 Poster for Dietrich & Company, 1898 HENRI MEUNIER

1902, the show emphasized a widespread commitment to progressive design and the democratization of art, goals explicitly linked with commerce. The postcard emerged as a worthy partner, embodying the intersecting goals of the internationalization of style and the popularization of design to attract a middle-class consumer audience.

Along with documenting artistic exchanges, the postcard highlights the international fluidity of style. For example, art nouveau, which has roots in Japanese art of the eighteenth century, traveled to Japan after 1900, in the form of postcards created by Japanese artists who first saw the new style at the Universal Exposition in Paris. Their work in turn influenced the development of Japanese art in the early decades of the twentieth century.[10]

As postcard artists plied their trade, finding stylistic and iconographic ways to vary tried and true themes—women, the months of the year, allegories, international capitals, dancers, beverages—they at once took cues from other artists (perhaps whose cards they received in the mail) and sought to make their own mark. The Hungarian artist Ilona Máté cre-

ated a series published in France that depicts tartan-clad figures of prim nannies walking with children and men smoking pipes—making clear why one of the terms for art nouveau was *le style anglais* (the English style) [62–63]. Another group of cards was created by the Polish artist Franciszek Laskowski, who became known as Franz Laskoff, one of the most representative artists of *Stile Liberty* in Italy. The silhouetted and cropped figures are familiar from the Viennese style, but their chic urbanity betrays the artist's Parisian training [64–65]. Publishers often reissued cards that were popular in another city; it is not uncommon to find postcards from the same set with backs in different languages and different publisher's imprints, showing the many iterations a popular set could go through.

While some cards blur stylistic and national boundaries, others demonstrate a sense of national pride, often through pointed declarations of difference. A series by the Hungarian artist Árpád Basch sets fashionably dressed ladies in ornamented architectural surrounds. The tightly corseted women wear local variants of the latest clothing style, while above them hover golden coats of arms or other symbols that identify each one's country of origin [69–70]. In turn, Basch's compatriot Jószef Divéky created a series of cards for a Zurich exhibition of decorative arts that is deeply rooted in folk forms, reflecting the interest of Hungarian designers in traditional life as an emblem of national identity [67–68]. The Russian Ivan Bilibin featured distinctive historical costumes on his postcards, elements that came to life in designs for a production by the impresario Serge Diaghilev [73–74]. Costumes inspired by Bilibin's illustrations helped establish the sense of authentic and luxurious exoticism that made Diaghilev's ballets all the rage in Paris.

While critics repeatedly mentioned the high quality of German cards, most often because artists there capitalized on the excellent printing capabilities of publishers, Belgian cards were most frequently cited for their outstanding artistic value. Dietrich & Company, a Brussels art publishing house, commissioned a line of postcards by members of the Belgian avant-

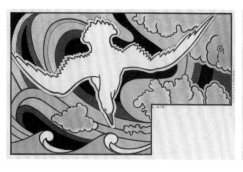

51–53 The elements, 1898 GISBERT COMBAZ

garde, including Henri Cassiers, Gisbert Combaz, Henri Meunier, and Victor Mignot, beginning in 1898. Dietrich publicized the postcard series (of which at least a dozen are known) with a poster by Meunier that depicts two figures looking into the window of its shop, the foremost fine art book and print store in Brussels [50]. The Dietrich series, which the publisher advertised in its catalogue for a decade, put Belgium on the postcard map, and turn-of-the-century exhibitions featured the series prominently. International publishers, such as Stopanni Fratelli in Milan, added the Dietrich cards to their inventories, likely hoping to spur local production as well as consumption of artists' postcards. British writers noted with envy that the participation of Belgium's best artists in the Dietrich project put the company at the forefront of postcard production.[11] Meunier created two series for Dietrich, including a striking tricolor *Zodiac* set, with starkly outlined forms printed in metallic ink, set against a starry midnight-blue sky that stands out from the orange-red frame. The series demonstrates everything that made Dietrich postcards sought after by collectors: impeccable quality, up-to-the-moment design, and serial production to encourage purchase of the complete set [75–76].

The three series by Combaz garnered the most attention for Dietrich. Combaz was repeatedly singled out for his distinctive and witty style in the spate of articles about artists' cards that appeared around the turn of the century. A quintessential art nouveau artist, Combaz derived his forms from abstracted nature. His particular brand of stylization refers overtly to Japanese design, with inventive cropping, strong forms, intense colors, and stark contours that suggest to today's viewer the psychedelic art of the 1960s more than the delicate lines and curves of European art nouveau. One critic asserted that Combaz's postcard series *The Elements* rose above "the flood of mediocrities" by its clever compositions and bold color contrasts [51–53, 77–79].[12] The Stoppani brothers similarly praised Combaz's *Elements* for the audacious symbolism and strange forms that they found "profoundly moving" and that they hoped would make the cards best sellers among Italian collectors.[13] Combaz stood out even to his detractors. The eminent German print historian Max Lehrs considered Belgian cards especially problematic in their form and taste, and stated that Combaz's postcards in particular were "downright ridiculous."[14]

Combaz, an outspoken promoter of artistic reform, would have welcomed such a judgment. The postcard was one of several media in which he worked, including posters, ceramics, and wallpaper, believing that art was not just for the wealthy. Trained originally as a lawyer and later a renowned scholar of Asian art, Combaz taught graphic arts and wrote art criticism that promoted the decorative arts. For him, postcards were more than a mere sideline or moneymaker; they were part of a passionate life project to transform quotidian existence through the democ-

STYLE

68

ratization of art. In championing the decorative arts, Combaz made no divisions between high and low, between commercial and fine art; indeed, he believed that artists' forays into the so-called lesser art forms could lead to "artistic rebirth."[15]

Alfonse Mucha, a master of the art nouveau style, capitalized on the postcard's qualities by having his Parisian poster publisher, Champenois, reissue many of his large-scale designs as postcards. He also created a couple of original series himself. Despite the efforts of Mucha, Combaz, and their comrades in the art nouveau revolution, postcards never became completely accepted as a form of high art. The English artist and critic Frank L. Emanuel noted in 1903 that French artists' cards were "hardly as important as might be expected."[16] Yet the postcard continues to offer opportunities for rediscovering forgotten artists who may have found their métier in the medium; we may even stumble upon the occasional lesser master like Combaz, whose postcards far outshine those by the more eminent Mucha.

At the turn of the century, the postcard provided fertile ground for visual experimentation, as artists forged new styles that would leave the past behind in order to revitalize contemporary design and everyday life. These small bits of paper became miniature works of art—both bona fide moneymakers and portable manifestos of style—that document the convergence of two phenomena emblematic of this exciting moment in time: the postcard and art nouveau.   L.K.

1. August Endell, "The Beauty of Form and Decorative Art," in *Art in Theory: An Anthology of Changing Ideas 1900– 2000*, ed. Charles Harrison and Paul Wood (Malden, Mass.: Wiley-Blackwell, 2009), 59–60. Originally published in *Dekorative Kunst* 1 (1897–98): 75–77, 119–25.

2. See Henry van de Velde, *Déblaiement d'art: suivi de, La triple offense à la beauté, Le nouveau, Max Elskamp, La voie sacrée, La colonne* (Bruxelles: Editions des Archives d'architecture moderne, 1979).

3. See Paul Greenhalgh, ed., *Art Nouveau 1890–1914*, exh. cat. (London: Victoria and Albert Museum, 2000); Giovanni Fanelli and Ezio Godoli, *Art Nouveau Postcards* (Oxford: Phaidon, 1987).

4. See Elisabeth Schmuttermeier and Christian Witt-Dörring, eds., *Postcards of the Wiener Werkstätte: A Catalogue Raisonné; Selections from the Leonard A. Lauder Collection* (Ostfildern: Hatje Cantz, 2010), 18–19.

5. See *Ein Dokument deutscher Kunst: Darmstadt, 1901–1976*, vol. 5, exh. cat. (Darmstadt: E. Roether, 1976).

6. H.W.S., "Studio Talk," *The International Studio: An Illustrated Magazine of Fine and Applied Art* 5 (1898): 287; *The International Studio* 6 (1899): 143.

7. "Petite chronique," *L'art moderne: Revue critique des arts et de la littérature* 18, no. 31 (July 31, 1898): 249.

8. Aldo Maggioni, "La 1.ª esposizione internazionale di cartoline postali illustrate a Venezia: Note ed appunti," *Emporium* 10 (1899): 314–16.

9. Frank L. Emanuel, "Pictorial Postcards: A General Survey," *The Magazine of Art*, n.s. 1 (1903): 91.

10. See Anne Nishimura Morse et al., *Art of the Japanese Postcard: The Leonard A. Lauder Collection at the Museum of Fine Arts Boston*, exh. cat. (Boston: Museum of Fine Arts, 2004), esp. 18–23.

11. Emanuel, "Pictorial Postcards," 89; F[ernand] K[hnopff], "Studio Talk," *The International Studio* 8, no. 32 (October 1899): 287.

12. "Petite chronique," 241.

13. Rossana Bossaglia, Ezio Godoli, and Marco Rosci, eds., *Torino 1902: Le arti decorative internazionali del nuovo secolo*, exh. cat. (Turin: Fabbri Editori, 1994), 233.

14. Max Lehrs, "Kuenstlerpostkarten," *Pan* 4, no. 3 (1898): 192.

15. Gisbert Combaz, "Les arts décoratifs au salon de la libre esthétique," *L'art moderne* 17, no. 13 (March 29, 1897): 97.

16. Emanuel, "Pictorial Postcards," 90.

54

54–55

Vienna Secession exhibition, 1898

KOLOMAN MOSER AND JOSEF HOFFMANN

56–57

Darmstadt Artists' Colony Exhibition, 1901

HANS CHRISTIANSEN

55

56

57

58

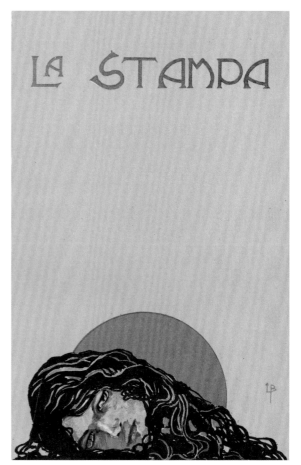

59

Photography, about 1900
LUIGI BOMPARD

58
Photography

59
The print

60
The lens

61
The negative

61

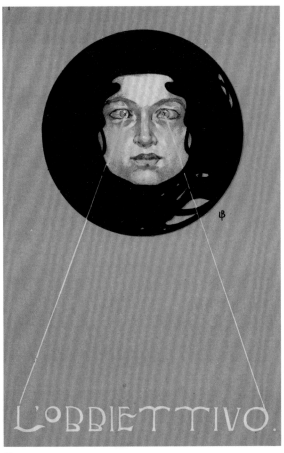

60

62

63

62–63
Fashionable people, about 1906
ILONA (HÉLÈNE) MÁTÉ

64–66

Months of the year, about 1900

FRANZ LASKOFF

64

65

66

67

67–68
Third Zurich Interior Design Show,
1911–12
JÓSZEF DIVÉKY

68

69

70

69–70

Women of the world, about 1900

ÁRPÁD BASCH

71

72

Russian epic poems, 1903
IVAN BILIBIN

71
Vol'ga

72
Sadko

73

74

Costumes for *Boris Godunov*, 1908

IVAN BILIBIN

73
A gentleman

74
A boyar

75–76

Signs of the zodiac, 1898

HENRI MEUNIER

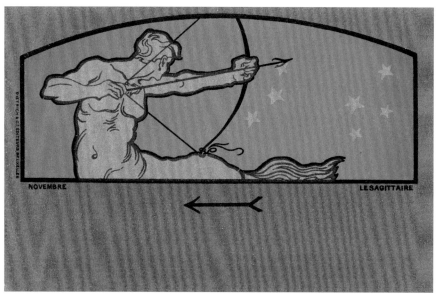

75

76

77–79

The elements, 1898

GISBERT COMBAZ

77

78

79

ABOUT TOWN

Yes, here we are, the grisettes
From Parisian cabarets . . .
Lolo! Dodo! Jou-Jou! Frou-Frou! Clo-Clo! Margot! And me!
Along the boulevard in the evening . . .
There we saunter, and we flirt,
We grisettes, back and forth!

— FRANZ LEHÁR, *The Merry Widow*, 1905

In 1900 Ernest Lessieux created a perfect, if slightly ridiculous, distillation of the delights of the city—at least from a man's point of view. A dapper gentleman, complete with top hat, monocle, and boutonnière, sits at a café table, enjoying a cigar and an aperitif. Couples stroll past in the background as they while away the evening. The gentleman's table holds two glasses, but there is no second chair; instead, as he sits and sips, his very own cancan girl helps pass the time. The image is from a series of postcards about dance through the ages. Each episode bears the image of a lovely lady who dances with, or sometimes for, a gentleman of a particular moment in history. While the other cards are labeled with eras or cultures— "Grecque," "Louis XIV," "Orientale"—this last one is titled simply "Moderne" [80].

The setting is clearly Paris: the big globular lights along the paths were trademarks of the city's Universal Exposition of 1900. But Lessieux's choice of this city as the essence of the modern was not just a matter of nationalist pride. A trendsetter in architecture and city planning, Paris was also an unparalleled urban playground, at the cutting edge of entertainment, leisure, and shifting social mores. And it was not just the Parisians who thought so. In 1905, when the Viennese operetta composer Franz Lehár took the characters of *The Merry Widow* from a remote Balkan kingdom to live the exciting big-city life, he sent them to Paris, not Vienna. It made for good theater: How could a young nobleman from the sticks resist the worldly bohemia of Lolo, Dodo, et al.—the world of the *grisettes*, the young, independent, and most certainly unconventional women who helped give Parisian nightlife its particular charm.

This world of boulevardiers and *café-concerts* was relatively new in 1900. It had grown up with the industrial cities of the nineteenth century, places that now seem the very essence of permanence and tradition, but were then raw and even disorienting environments that left visitors and residents alike searching for anchors in the past. History must have seemed to be slipping away very quickly, and it is telling that among the various make-believe African villages and Japanese pagodas that dotted world's fairs of the period, nearly every exposition also included a reconstruction of a long-ago version of the bustling industrial host city. The elaborate confection called "Le vieux Paris" that stretched along the Seine at the Universal Exposition even featured performances of medieval music and costumed vendors who hawked their wares with traditional street cries.[1]

80 Dance through the ages.
Moderne, 1900
ERNEST LOUIS LESSIEUX

Opposite:
81–82 Berlin sights, 1912.
Friedrichstrasse train station;
Potsdamer Platz in the evening
WALTER BUHE

Had the gentleman and the cancan girl in Lessieux's postcard visited that theme park, the experience would only have highlighted the sense of a huge distance between their world and old Paris. For one thing, industrialization had caused cities to become much bigger than ever before. Paris, long one of Europe's largest cities, grew from about a million people in the 1850s to more than two million in 1900; in the same decades, Budapest and Berlin almost tripled their populations, nearly matching the growth rates of newer, brasher places across the ocean like New York and Chicago. Cities throughout Europe and the Americas overleapt their traditional borders and spread out into the surrounding countryside, as dense and tangled city centers came to be ringed by factories, rail yards, and block after block of apartments and villas. In Vienna, the medieval city walls came down, and the empty space they left behind became a grand ring of boulevards lined by cultural institutions and residences. In Boston, a desire to create a miniature Paris gave birth to a tidy grid of avenues and streets on land wrested from the smelly tidal marsh called the Back Bay. And even in Rome, huge swaths of land north and east of the Colosseum

filled up with buildings for the first time since antiquity; the ancient sculptures that emerged from the excavations for their foundations filled several museums.[2]

Most of this urban growth came from migration. The same forces that drew millions to the United States in those decades pulled still greater numbers from Europe's countryside to its cities, as people relocated in search of work and money. In a phenomenon seen in places as diverse as Renaissance Florence and contemporary Bangkok, migrants from one town or region often settled in the same urban district, ensuring a certain amount of economic solidarity and social continuity. But the scale and complexity of the big cities ultimately broke down traditional patterns, pushing groups into contact whether they liked it or not, and leaving people to find their way in a universe whose social cues and roles were unmoored from tradition.

Some observers, such as the Berlin sociologist Georg Simmel, thought that cities had created a new sort of person, distinct from those who lived in smaller towns and earlier times. Less bound by interpersonal relationships than their country cousins, city people were colder and more calculating, yet

BAHNHOF FRIEDRICHSTRASSE

POTSDAMER PLATZ AM ABEND

also helplessly subject to forces beyond their control. Simmel claimed that the anonymity of big cities—the sheer press of people—led to the cultivation of the "strangest eccentricities . . . of caprice, of fastidiousness, the meaning of which is no longer to be found in the content of such activity itself but rather in its being a form of 'being different'—of making oneself noticeable."[3] In short, the city itself created Lolo, Dodo, Jou-Jou, and Frou-Frou, the dandy at the table, and even the unnamed cancan girl in the postcard.

If being noticed was the goal, where better than on the boulevard, that quintessential metropolitan environment? As Lehar's *grisettes* knew, strolling was key to the urban experience. In postcards from the turn of the century, fashionable silhouettes walk the bridges of Dresden, looking out over the city's famous skyline

[85–86]. In Vienna, Raphael Kirchner's more fully realized strollers—"Viennese types"— process along the Ringstrasse's grand boulevards. They pause as if for snapshots in front of each of the Ring's great monuments: the opera, the parliament, and, just off the boulevard, the baroque Church of Saint Charles Borromeo, with its pair of spiral triumphal columns [88]. In another series, from Berlin, commuters and shoppers move busily through the city's frenetic downtown, as trams zip past and advertising signs light the night sky. These cards convey that the city is a spectacle in and of itself—a place you want to be [81–82].

Strolling is exercise—albeit of a gentle sort—but it is also a form of leisure. Here, too, cities presented something new and different. They grew because people came in search of work, but cities fostered new ways to spend free time as well. The growing middle class provided a mass audience for theater, spectacle, and recreation, and the slow but steady progress of reforms in working conditions meant that even factory workers had idle hours.[4] Towns of modest size often boasted several theaters, and large cities had dozens, neatly sorted by price and respectability. They presented operas and concerts and serious plays of the sort that have endured across the decades, but much of the era's energy and innovation actually found its expression in more lighthearted sorts of entertainment.

Dead and embalmed today, amusements like the variety show, the *café-concert*, vaudeville, and operetta were wildly alive at the turn of the century. Frothy operettas held the stage in every European and American city and appealed across a wide social spectrum. Operetta was light and fun, an easy way to pass the time, but it also provided society a safety valve. Despite plots that ran the gamut from frivolous and formulaic straight on to nonsensical, operetta could bring everyday life and social concerns directly onstage. The life-and-death struggles of the Nordic gods that Richard Wagner had conjured in his *Ring of the Nibelung* provided a high-minded aesthetic and emotional experience, but Oscar Straus's *Die lustigen Nibelungen* (The Merry Nibelungs), which places tongue directly in cheek to recast the hero Siegfried as an upper-middle-class sparkling-wine manufacturer, probably resonated with contemporary experience in ways Wagner's original could not.[5] And it was over in an hour and a half.

Like today's television programming, much of this entertainment was disposable. Theaters and theatergoers were ravenous for constant novelty, and for every play or operetta that has remained in the repertoire, hundreds have left only traces behind. One elegant postcard from Berlin advertises an operetta by Rudolf Báron called *Das Liebes-Sanatorium*—or, roughly, *The Love Hospital*. The show, about a health spa called the Sanatorium Spleen (a play on the French poet Charles Baudelaire's morbid celebration of mod-

ern urban life) sank like a stone after its 1912 premiere, granting the ephemeral postcard a greater presence in history than the operetta it advertised [99].

The Parisian scene was particularly bubbly. Paris had effectively invented the nightclub, and the city's most famous theaters and bawdy shows—the Moulin Rouge (The Red Mill), Le Divan Japonais (The Japanese Sofa), and the Folies Bergères (Shepherdess's Follies)—were known around the world. Even respectable visitors to Paris felt the need to experience a *café-concert*, nightclubs with live music, novelty acts, and (often very racy) dancing. Around 1900, the Moulin Rouge hired Charles Naillod to create a series of cards that featured a parade of cancan dancers, one per card, each framed by an audience and a reminder that the show went on every night at nine [89–90]. Easily distributed and just as easily hidden, postcards were an ideal advertising tool for such establishments.

Naillod was selling the whole experience of the Moulin Rouge, not promoting a particular dancer, but some performers became very famous indeed. In late 1901 the Société Industrielle de Photographie celebrated the excitement of Parisian theater with a lively postcard series in which stars seem to burst through the advertising posters for their current shows [91–94]. The cards include serious actresses from stages like the Comédie-Française, but also feature stars from the city's grander nightclubs and variety stages. The actresses are not always identified, but they probably did not need to be, as each one had a carefully crafted public personality. The singer Germaine Gallois, for example, was renowned for her stately and shapely figure—reinforced by a neck-to-waist corset so restrictive she refused any role that required her to sit down.[6]

Even the liveliest live theater is still a form of passive entertainment, and turn-of-the-century cities abounded in places for more active leisure as well. Nearly every city boasted fairgrounds, bowling alleys, dance halls, and skating rinks—both ice and roller. In Brussels, one of the most popular was the Bains de Saint-Sauveur, whose name suggests an aristocratic

83–84 The scenic railway at Luna Park, Paris, after 1909

resort, but which was actually a swimming pool, steam room, and dance hall just up the hill from the central station. Such pleasure palaces needed to keep up with the latest fads, so shortly after the turn of the century, the Bains installed underground bowling alleys and an ice rink. The lanes were not far from the king's palace, so they were dubbed, in fashionable English, Royal Bowling [95–96].[7]

Establishments like the Bains offered a full social experience, not just a place to swim or skate or bowl. When Berlin's first roller rink opened in 1909, it advertised with postcards that feature a fashionable three-some who stroll, skates dangling from their wrists, to the rink. There, the card promises, they will find "first-class attractions, artistic concerts, five o'clock teas, and exquisite food" along with the skating. Whether or not the reality lived up to these promises, the proprietor, an American trick cyclist named Nick Kaufmann, did express hope that he could attract Germany's crown prince as a guest, since the prince had shown interest in ice skating [100].[8]

The ultimate form of packaged leisure was the amusement park, another invention of the age. Like postcards, parks crossed national borders. Take Luna Park as an example. In 1903, two entrepreneurs—a money and operations man named Skip Dundy and the architect Frederick Thompson—bought a tract of

land on Coney Island, already a popular leisure-time destination for New Yorkers. They gave the name Luna Park to their thirty-six-acre "electric Baghdad," built on the principle that "people are just boys and girls grown tall." It offered a safe, clean, and family-friendly escape from the city, featuring novelty rides such as "A Trip to the Moon" and ethnographic displays, all arrayed around a pool like the artificial lakes that often graced world's fairs—except that this one culminated in a giant waterslide. The park was an immediate success, attracting four million visitors in 1904 [108–109].[9]

Over the next few years, Luna Parks opened throughout Europe. Whether in Berlin, Paris, or Vienna, the imitators shared many features with the original, though perhaps not its epic ambition. The Paris version opened in 1909, offering, among other diversions, a dance hall, a "mysterious river," a scenic railway that went over "Pike's Peak," a wobbly ride called the "devil's wheels," and the iconic water slide [83–84].[10] Constant novelty was essential to keep customers coming back. In New York, rides changed frequently and new exhibits refreshed the experience each year. The Luna Park in Paris hosted the start of the Tour de France bicycle race in 1912, and in June 1914 welcomed crowds that witnessed the African American boxer Jack Johnson's defense of the world heavyweight title. Berlin's version opened in 1910, preceded by an advertising campaign that commanded "every Berliner at least once to Luna Park." It nearly succeeded, as the park had more than one million visitors in its first two months.[11]

Unlike today's amusement parks, these establishments did not always stand alone. Berlin's Luna Park was right on the Kurfürstendamm, the major thoroughfare in the prosperous and quickly growing western part of the city, just a few doors down from Nick Kaufmann's roller rink. Vienna's version, which opened in 1910, was built into the city's permanent fairgrounds just north of the famous park known as the Prater [110–111]. The area had first been set aside for the city's international exposition in 1873, and Luna Park debuted as part of the International Hunting Exhibition, a sort of world's fair that gathered animal- and hunting-themed memorabilia from around the world. The show's organizers considered the amusement park enough of a draw to include several scenes of its delights among the fair's official postcards; yet they excluded it almost completely from the exhibition's memorial publication. In that gigantic book, replete with tables of statistics and alarming pictures of the fair's antler-filled pavilions, Luna Park appears only once, at the edge of the map. No pictures, no descriptions. Yet the exhibition lasted only a summer; Luna Park survived for decades.[12]   B.W.

1. Edward N. Kaufman, "The Architectural Museum from World's Fair to Restoration Village," *Assemblage* 9 (1989): 20–39; David Frisby, *Cityscapes of Modernity: Critical Explorations* (Cambridge: Polity, 2001), 104–7.

2. John Lukacs, *Budapest 1900: A Historical Portrait of a City and Its Culture* (New York: Weidenfeld and Nicolson, 1988), 68–69, 72–73.

3. Georg Simmel, "The Metropolis and Mental Life," in *The Blackwell City Reader*, ed. Gary Bridge and Sophie Watson, 2nd ed. (Oxford: Blackwell, 2010), 105, 109.

4. Gary S. Cross, *A Quest for Time: The Reduction of Work in Britain and France, 1840–1940* (Berkeley: University of California Press), esp. chaps. 2 and 3.

5. Charles Rearick, *Pleasures of the Belle Epoque: Entertainment and Festivity in Turn-of-the-Century France* (New Haven: Yale University Press, 1985); Peter Hanák, "The Cultural Role of the Vienna-Budapest Operetta," in *The Garden and the Workshop: Essays on the Cultural History of Vienna and Budapest* (Princeton: Princeton University Press, 1998): 135–46; Peter Jelavich, "Modernity, Civic Identity, and Metropolitan Entertainment: Vaudeville, Cabaret, and Revue in Berlin, 1901–1933," in *Berlin: Culture and Metropolis*, ed. Charles W. Haxthausen and Heidrun Suhr (Minneapolis: University of Minnesota Press, 1990), 96.

6. Eugen Weber, *France: Fin de Siècle* (Cambridge, Mass.: Harvard University Press, 1986), 103.

7. *http://sofei-vandenaemet.skynetblogs.be/archive/2008/01/08/saint-sauveur.html* (accessed 10/26/ 2011).

8. "Berlin's American Rink," *New York Times*, May 30, 1909, C4.

9. Gary S. Cross and John K. Walton, *The Playful Crowd: Pleasure Places in the Twentieth Century* (New York: Columbia University Press), 40–42; Frederic Thompson, "Amusing the Million," *Everybody's Magazine* 19, no. 3 (September 1908): 378–87.

10. Gilles-Antoine Langlois, *Folies, Tivolis et attractions: Les premiers parcs de loisirs parisiens* (Paris: Delegation à l'action artistique de la Ville de Paris [1991]): 60–62, 69.

11. Peter Fritzsche, *Reading Berlin 1900* (Cambridge, Mass.: Harvard University Press, 1996): 67; Roger Green, "The City and Entertainment: Coney Island and Haus Vaterland," in *Berlin—New York: Like and Unlike: Essays on Architecture and Art from 1870 to the Present*, ed. Josef Paul Kleihues and Christina Rathgeber (New York: Rizzoli, 1993), 216.

12. *Die Erste International Jagd-Ausstellung, Wien 1910: Ein monumentales Gedenkbuch* (Vienna: Frick, 1912). See also *wwwg.uni-klu.ac.at/kultdoku/kataloge/03/html/348.htm* (accessed 10/26/2011).

85

86

Dresden street scenes, about 1900

85
View from the Carolus bridge

86
The old city with the Augustus bridge

87–88

Viennese types, 1897–99

RAPHAEL KIRCHNER

87

88

91

89

Women of the Paris stage, 1901

91
Armande Cassive

92
Marthe Brandès

93
Jeanne Bloch (?)

94
Germaine Gallois

89–90
The Moulin Rouge, about 1905
CHARLES NAILLOD

90

91

92

93

94

Bains de Saint-Sauveur,
Brussels, about 1910

S. BAILIE

95

96

97

98

97–98

Poster Views of New York, 1924

99
The Love Hospital.
Burlesque operetta
by Rudolf Báron,
1912
GEORG CARÉ

100
Roller skating rink,
about 1910
FRITZ RUMPF

99

100

101
Grand Café Schöneberg,
about 1914
MICHEL NOA

102
Trocadero. Hamburg's most
genteel establishment,
about 1910
FRITZ RUMPF

101

102

103

103–104

Sarrasani Circus, about 1928

105–107

The Basel zoo, about 1922

HEDWIG KEERL THOMA

104

105

106

107

108

108–109
Hold-to-light cards of
Luna Park, Coney Island,
about 1910

109

110

111

110–111

Luna Park, Vienna, 1910

HANS KALMSTEINER

WOMEN

Why not the eternal male for a change?

— JEROME K. JEROME,
The Angel and the Author—And Others, 1908

In turn-of-the-century London, Dorothy Levitt cut an impressive figure. Known for dressing in the most fashionable clothes, she was on the A-list for all of the city's premier events, hosted famous luncheon parties at her home, and could be found at the horse races at Ascot or regattas at Henley, as the season demanded. She moved easily in both the "sacred circles of society" and the bohemian sphere alongside artists, writers, and musicians, according to the author of a biographical sketch. Miss Levitt also boasted some unusual accomplishments: England's first female professional race car driver, she set the world's speed record for a woman in 1906 and again the following year, earning the description "the fastest girl on earth." She was also a motorboat-racing champion, winning at Cowes on the Isle of Wight in 1903, where King Edward VII congratulated her personally. So remarkable were Miss Levitt's achievements that one might expect her to be a "big, strapping Amazon." Indeed, her defining characteristics seemed to be her fiercely competitive nature and independence. Her biographer reassured his readers, however, that she was graceful, slim, and charming, "the most girlish of womanly women," and, perhaps more important, bashful and

modest to a fault.[1] Such were the contradictions facing the modern *fin de siècle* woman.

The occasion for the biographical essay was the publication in 1909 of Dorothy Levitt's own book, *The Woman and the Car: A Chatty Little Handbook for Women Who Motor or Want to Motor*. Her guide was intended to entice women to experience firsthand the "intense pleasure" of driving, which multiplied "the delights of the gallop." She gave advice on everything from the best car to buy to how to change the oil or make roadside repairs. She warned her readers that they would need to have "a capacity for taking pains" if they were to become drivers and instructed them to carry a small revolver for protection on the roads. But she also devoted an entire chapter to proper dress, suggesting that women drivers keep a powder puff next to the revolver in the glove box, to help them avoid looking "horrendous" after a drive.[2]

Levitt was just one of countless trailblazing women of her time who embraced the new freedoms brought by technology, increased working opportunities, and changing social norms. Postcards, whose craze coincided with this moment of burgeoning female emancipation, often depict women in these newly public roles, riding bicycles or driving motor cars [114]. Series of photographic postcards of Paris included new urban types, such as female poster hangers and taxi drivers [117–120].[3] Whereas itinerant street vendors like the knife grinder represented the disappearing traditions of old Paris, these workingwomen signaled the changing and vibrant city of the new century. Even as women participated in the transformation of daily life, however, they had to negotiate codes of behavior, rules of decorum, and social expectations that remained in place.

These developments called forth numerous tracts and treatises questioning women's role in society and commenting on the expansion of their civil rights. Many sought to reconcile the benefits of women's expanding freedoms with challenges to their traditional roles as mothers and domestic caregivers. A conservative writer such as the British eugenicist C. W. Saleeby could give lukewarm endorsement to the women's reform movement by arguing that expanded education and even the vote would help women to be better mothers—the primary occupation that they should not desert. At the other end of the spectrum, the Austrian feminist Rosa Mayreder stated in her 1913 book *A Survey of the Woman Problem* that the woman's movement was one of the few honorable aspects of an otherwise depraved era. She added that its proponents should nonetheless remember that women were not the equal of men in strength of will, a character trait necessitated by their natural predestination to bear children and their need to be susceptible to "sexual conquest."[4]

Even lesser-knowns chimed in, like one Alice E. Major, who gave a lecture in Brussels in 1898 in which she rebutted the characteristics of the "ideal woman" she had recently found in a book by an unnamed male author. Traditional qualities like beauty, sweetness, timidity, resignation, sentimentality, chastity, and modesty, she argued, had given way to a woman who is "strong, brilliant and happy, helpful and confident in herself" and "the infallible champion of the oppressed."[5] Lectures of this sort were given throughout Europe and the United States in conjunction with international women's congresses, the first of which was held at the time of the 1878 Universal Exposition in Paris. The body of academic writing that developed on the subject was extensive and diverse, and it brought to the fore the main source of tension in the women's movement. As the editor of the 1911 German publication *Ruf an die Frauen* (Call to Women) dryly noted, when men wrote about the women's movement, they seemed to have "greater concern for their own sovereign rights than for those of women." Even texts by the "feisty daughters of Eve" seemed to inspire more concern for their husbands' dignity than for their own.[6]

Anxieties about changing gender roles are also revealed on postcards. The image of suffragists as unattractive and overbearing was particularly popular. Several postcard series of such women endorsed this view, sometimes suggesting that the solution to the suffragist problem was, simply, the muzzle [121–124]. Such postcards, and similar images in other popular media, reflected the concern that as the woman earned the vote or started to work, the man would become feminized, condemned to household chores or even to staying at home to nurse the children. In turn, these women were characterized as somehow unfeminine and unnatural, dominating their meek and cowering husbands.

Magazines for a less academic audience took a gentler approach to the woman problem. *La femme et le monde* (The Woman and the World), for example, stated in its first issue in 1901 that its aim was to provide readers with guidelines for being a "real" French woman—the ideal of women around the world—who knows how to "distinguish good taste from bad taste" and "fears the tawdry and the indiscreet." The magazine offered the latest refined novels, drawings, fashions, and musical scores. It also included photographic spreads with beautiful women modeling the proper smile for a range of emotions—from playful to innocent to melancholic—or demonstrating acceptable gestures to convey perplexity, expectation, or modesty.[7]

Postcards often echoed conservative publications like these in bestowing upon women an array of characteristics that made them acceptable to traditionalists and offered an antidote to the intimidating new women. For an artist such as Raphael Kirchner,

the female body provided a template for the seemingly endless variations that publishers craved to feed the addiction of collectors. Kirchner's signature type was a delicate and malleable female form, which he adapted in various guises and set in different historical moments, in series with titles like *Fleurs d'amour* (Flowers of love) and *Fruits douces* (Sweet fruits). In this fantasy world, lush and willing ladies pose to display their assets for the delectation of male viewers. Coyly demure and exceptionally feminine, they would have been at home on the pages of *La femme et le monde* [112].

These alluring and sexualized miniature ladies could be slipped into a man's pocket to await a surreptitious glance or be proudly housed in an album to serve as models of dress and behavior. The containable postcard woman could also embody the bawdy side of modern urban life. Octave Uzanne, a conservative chronicler of French society and self-appointed arbiter of taste, opined that the Parisian woman was superior to all others because the city gave her "a high degree of attractiveness, the delicacy, the coquetry, the magic seductiveness of certain hothouse flowers, specially cultivated for our hours of pleasure."[8] The *petites femmes* who appeared on postcards also proliferated in risqué publications such as *La vie Parisienne* (Parisian Life), advancing the image of Paris as a city of desire and intoxications of all kinds. A series of *Parisian Sights* from 1905 shows such lively ladies suggestively mounting the city's most prominent monuments, giving a new meaning to tourist attractions like the Place de l'Etoile [129–131].

Postcard artists, overwhelmingly male, expressed desire of all kinds through the female body, transforming it in multiple ways. Some indulged in bawdy visual puns. More sophisticated artists, including early users of photomontage, thoughtfully compiled source material to titillate recipients. To reassure the male audience of dominance during this time of rapid change, several artists created series depicting tiny men gleefully conquering the peaks and valleys of anthropomorphized mountains, with names like the *Jungfrau*

112 Flowers of love, about 1900 RAPHAEL KIRCHNER

(virgin) that lent themselves to double meaning [132–136]. Postcard advertisements were also among the first to imply that the purchase of a beer or a new car included the acquisition of a lovely female as well.

Such images of sweetly sensual objects of desire countered the threat posed by real women who were breaking out of traditional roles. Whether she was a *neue Frau, femme nouvelle,* or New Woman, she challenged norms of femininity by daring to wear her hair short, ride a bike, or even smoke or drink in public. The early decades of the twentieth century saw a corresponding reform movement in fashion that sought, according to one advocate, "a new type of women's clothing, which would not be harmful to

LA QUESTION EST POSEE : *portera-t-on la jupe-pantalon en 1911 ? ?*
Présentée à la Comédie-Française à la Générale d' « Après moi »,

113 At Auteuil, discussing fashion, 1911

health, and would allow greatest flexibility . . . and bring out the [natural] forms of the body."[9] Beyond escape from the tight corsets and awkwardly proportioned clothing into which women routinely squeezed their anatomies, this movement reflected women's increasing public participation in sports like tennis or skating. Decorum and neatness of appearance were still prized over functionality; one writer noted in reference to women's wearing bloomers: "Men do not object in the least, so long as the touch of femininity, of modesty, is never lost."[10] Such developments often eased society into jarring changes. At the height of the bicycle craze of the late 1890s, only the most daring women donned baggy trousers or bloomers, sometimes creating controversy in cities and towns throughout Europe and North America. Within fifteen years, a postcard series depicting the fashion-forward types who socialized at the Auteuil

racecourse could ask about the fashion for culottes: "Will they wear the *jupe-pantalon* in 1911?" [113].[11]

The depiction of women on postcards was not the sole province of male artists. Because the postcard was considered a minor art, it also provided an opportunity for women to work as professional artists. Among the most successful was the Viennese artist Mela Koehler, trained at the city's Kunstgewerbeschule (school of arts and crafts) and the Wiener Werkstätte (Viennese Workshops) in typical female genres like textile design and ceramics. She became the most prolific artist for the Workshops' extensive postcard series and produced hundreds of designs for other Austrian postcard publishers such as M. Munk and Brüder Kohn as well. Like Kirchner, Koehler created a signature style that depicted sweet and attractive women, although less sexualized than his. Koehler's ladies, stylish and sporting women of the day rather than otherworldly fantasies, reflect their creator's interest in textiles as well as her illustration work for fashion magazines [141–144].

As a postcard subject, the field of fashion especially highlighted the push and pull between modernity and tradition, the adventurous and the familiar, felt by women as they constructed their own public images. Even as women sought less restrictive clothing, opulence, display, and femininity remained priorities—expressed in the increasing power of women as middle-class consumers. Emphasis on impossibly small corseted waists was superseded by attention to accessories such as the oversized muffs and collars, enticing to the touch, found in a stunning set of black-and-white fashion postcards from Salzburg around 1920. Fashionable women at Auteuil, in turn, sported coquettish parasols in a series of photographic postcards from 1912 [145–150].

Perhaps no postcards better conjure the stakes of high fashion than those from a humor series entitled *Le Sourire* (The Smile), made by André-Félix Roberty in 1909. Roberty took aim at the way hats, which were signifiers of style, social status, and modesty, grew bigger and bigger during the first decades of the twentieth century. Piled high with not only flowers, feathers, bows, and gauze, but also stuffed birds and velvet vegetables, and sporting ever wider brims, hats took on humorous names like the "Merry Widow" or the "flower pot." A fashion critic remarked that by 1908 hats had become "show-places for curios" whose enormous brims extended "half-way down the block" and "compelled architects to modify their plans of space and structure." She further reported that a group of progressive sophomore coeds at the University of Chicago demanded the proscription of such hats, considering them "a psychic phenomenon of the feminine temperament when irrationally inclined."[12] In Roberty's series, those who succumbed to this trend become mere pedestals for such extravagant creations, which, in his fantastical world, sometimes even offer cover for naughty activities [151–154].

Such fashion developments proved a boon to publishers who sought to add to the supply of postcards they made available to collectors. As the humorist Jerome K. Jerome noted in 1908, "The dealer has fallen back upon the eternal feminine. The postcard collector is confined to girls. Through the kindness of correspondents I possess myself some fifty to a hundred girls, or perhaps it would be more correct to say one girl in fifty to a hundred different hats. I have her in big hats, I have her in small hats, I have her in no hat at all. I have her smiling, and I have her looking as if she had lost her last sixpence. I have her overdressed, I have her decidedly underdressed, but she is much the same girl."

Postcards faithfully document the contradictions of woman's societal place and behavioral norms at the *fin de siècle*. For the most part, they promoted the image of an unrealistic and unthreatening ideal woman, sexualized but contained. As Jerome pointed out, reality and fantasy did not necessarily coincide: "Nature, in fashioning women, has not yet crept up to the artistic ideal. The young man studies the picture on the postcard . . . and thinks with discontent of Polly Perkins, who in a natural way is as pretty a girl as can be looked for in this imperfect world. Thus it is that woman has had to take to shorthand and typewriting. Modern woman is being ruined by the artist."[13]   L.K.

1. C. Byng-Hall, "Dorothy Levitt: A Personal Sketch," introduction to Dorothy Levitt, *The Woman and the Car: A Chatty Little Handbook for Women Who Motor or Want to Motor* (London: John Lane, 1909), 3–12.
2. Levitt, *The Woman and the Car*, 16, 15, 30, 23, 28.
3. See Naomi Schor, "*Cartes Postales*: Representing Paris 1900," *Critical Inquiry* 18 (Winter 1992): 188–241.
4. C. W. Saleeby, *Woman and Womanhood: A Search for Principles* (New York: Mitchell Kennerley, 1911), 23; Rosa Mayreder, *A Survey of the Woman Problem*, trans. Herman Scheffauer (New York: George H. Doran Company, 1913), 39.
5. Alice E. Major, *La femme idéal: Conférence donnée le 25 Janvier 1898 à la salle Ravenstein, à Bruxelles*, 12–16.
6. "Allgemeine Beobachtungen," in *Ruf an die Frauen* (Berlin: W. Kästner, 1911), 7.
7. "A nos lectrices" and "La grace éloquente et variée du sourire," *La femme et le monde* 1, no. 1 (October 5, 1901): 2, 8–9; "La grace du geste féminine," *La femme et le monde* 1, no. 3 (October 19, 1901): 34–35.
8. Octave Uzanne, *The Modern Parisienne* (New York: Putnam, 1912), 2, originally published in French in 1894 as *La femmes à Paris: Nos contemporaines.*
9. "Anatomische Grundlage zur Frauenkleidung," *Ruf an die Frauen*, 70–71.
10. See *www3.fitnyc.edu/museum/sporting_life/early_gym_suit.html* (accessed 1/26/2012).
11. See David V. Herlihy, *Bicycle: The History* (New Haven: Yale University Press, 2004), 267–72.
12. Izola Forrester, "The Marvelous Hats of 1908," *Munsey's Magazine* 39, no. 4 (July 1908): 519–24.
13. Jerome K. Jerome, *The Angel and the Author—And Others* (London: Hurst and Blackett, 1908), 92–93, 94.

114

114
Motoring
M.C.

115
In the library
M.C.

116
Late autumn
M.C.

MODERN STYLE.

115

MODERN STYLE.

116

Les premières femmes colleuses d'affiches

117

926. - La première Femme colleuse d'affiches

J. H.

118

117–118
Paris's first women poster hangers, about 1908

119–120
Women taxi drivers in Paris, about 1908

PARIS MODERNE — CHAUFFEUSE D'AUTOTAX
Contravention pour excès de vitesse au Bois
2898   *Activée par un client pressé, notre pauvre Chauffeuse n'a pu échapper à la vigilance d'un garde ;*
une contravention va lui rappeler qu'au Bois l'allure doit être modérée

ND Phot.

119

PARIS MODERNE — CHAUFFEUSE D'AUTOTAX, LA MISE EN MARCHE
En lui voyant prendre la manivelle, vous craignez pour elle
le retour en arrière. Soyez sans inquiétude, ses nerfs sont d'acier,
2892   *elle saura passer la compression et allumer du premier coup*

120

121

Women wearing muzzles, before 1914

121
Muzzle or no muzzle, jabber she will!

122
"It's a good job for you I can't get at you!"

123
A solution of the suffragette question!

124
This animal is quite harmless if not touched!

122

123

124

125

126

125–126

Around Paris, about 1900–1910

FRANÇOIS XAVIER SAGER

A VALENTINE
MESSAGE

127

VALENTINE
GREETING

128

127–128
Valentine postcards, about 1900

129

Parisian sights, 1905

C. FOX

129
Le Sacré Coeur

130
Place de l'Etoile

131
The Great Wheel

131

130

132

133

132
Two men and a woman, about 1900

133
A man and a woman, about 1900

134
The Jungfrau, about 1900

135–136
Neckties, about 1912

134

135

136

137–139

Continental Pneumatic,
about 1900

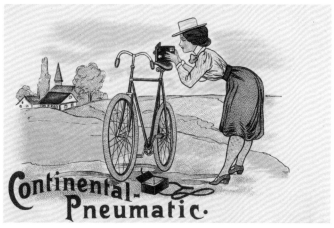

137

138

139

Ich weiss ja doch, was Dich erquickt,
Drum sei Dir dieses heut geschickt.
Nun, lieber Freund, ich wünsche Dir
Von ganzem Herzen

Ich weiss ja doch, was Dich erquickt,
Drum sei Dir dieses heut geschickt.
Nun, lieber Freund, ich wünsche Dir
Von ganzem Herzen

„Prosit" hier!

140
"Cheers!" beer mug

141

141–142

Women modeling hats, about 1910

MELA KOEHLER

143–144

Women with small dogs, about 1910

MELA KOEHLER

142

143

144

Blanche-noir.

145

Blanche-noir.

146

145–148

Fashion in "white-black," 1920s

Blanche-noir.

147

Blanche-noir.

148

ND Phot.

1 — Champ de Courses d'AUTEUIL. — Au Paddock. Toilettes d'Eté.

149

149–150

At Auteuil, 1912

151–154

Fashion in 1909

ANDRÉ-FÉLIX ROBERTY

7 — Champ de Courses d'AUTEUIL. — Devant les Tribunes.
Toilettes d'Eté.   ND Phot.

150

WOMEN

151

152

153

154

EDOUARD VII

FAMOUS AND FAMILIAR

So, the king of Portugal has censured postcards ridiculing his corpulence; in the Netherlands, the post is ordered to intercept cards bearing the likeness of the former Queen Draga . . . or that of Prince Henry of Holland. Germany aims to ban cards bearing the image of Tolstoy.

— *Le collectionneur,* January 10, 1906

Every era has famous people, whether celebrated or notorious, who define it. The modern cult of celebrity—with its constant public performances for the media that feed it—emerged with the nineteenth-century explosion of print culture. From woodcuts in penny broadsheets to fine engravings sold in portfolios, from tabloids to literary journals, reproducible and commercial mass media shrank the space between public and private. The barrage of images of powerful or famous people made the instantly recognizable celebrity at once a constant source of public fodder and a defining element of modernity.

Among these mass media images, postcards offered a key ingredient in the making of celebrity— serial publication. Publishers and artists could supply numerous variations on a single theme to whet and then satisfy the public's thirst for images of the famous. They placed political figures and royalty, among the most represented celebrity figures in the postcard format, in an endless variety of invented scenarios—from battle scenes to the latest popular amusements—often in humorous or less than respectful guises. The physical attributes of the famous, such as the ample girth of figures like Carlos I of Portugal, Edward VII of England, and the U.S. president William Taft, offered artists ammunition for ridicule, which proved popular with postcard collectors [161]. And Carlos I's censure of satirical postcard representations of himself indicates that they did not go unheeded by their subjects either.

The malleability of celebrity—from royalty to stage actors—made it one of the most popular collecting categories during the postcard craze. Some contemporary critics thought that celebrity cards especially represented the negative popularizing aspects of the postcard and confirmed a lamentable cultural decline.[1] After all, what respectable person of culture needed to document the demimonde of Parisian theater by collecting a postcard of every one of Sarah Bernhardt's roles, or of each actress who graced a stage in the city on the night of December 23, 1901? Defenders of the postcard instead saw the amassing of celebrity postcards as a sign of the medium's relevance to the moment, dubbed by one observer the "view and . . . actress epoch."[2]

Celebrity cards fed particularly well into the human impulse to arrange and order that made postcards such a successful phenomenon for producers and consumers alike. In 1899, the Italian critic Aldo Maggioni noted in his review of the collectors' section at the postcard exhibition in Venice: "Everything has been properly classified and divided by countries,

155 Wilhelm II, emperor of Germany, 1903
GEO (HENRI JULES JEAN GEOFFROY)

156 The Shah of Persia, 1903
GEO (HENRI JULES JEAN GEOFFROY)

styles, authors, subjects."[3] Some three decades later, the same impulse was the target of a publicity campaign by London's National Portrait Gallery, which issued four hundred cards in a series depicting the most important British figures in its collection. A newspaper account pointed out the particular suitability of postcards—and especially those bearing celebrity images—to such activities: "With a little shuffling . . . the happy possessor can reconstruct a fascinating

gallery: indeed by permutations . . . he can rig up a perpetual variety of exhibitions in miniature . . . now [by] date, now profession, now sex . . . The cards are much more obedient to their owner's whim than the pictures on the wall can be to the visitor, and they invite more human treatment."[4]

An immediate precedent for the celebrity postcard was the photographic *carte-de-visite*, or calling card, which first circulated among people of means in the mid-nineteenth century. Uniform in size and format like the postcard, the *carte-de-visite* contained a photographic portrait of the bearer. The collecting audience for these cards expanded as photography became more affordable. Photographers rushed to supply the demand and issued *carte-de-visite* series of celebrities ranging from royals such as Napoleon III and his wife Eugénie to provocatively posed dance-hall girls. Napoleon even encouraged the circulation of his cards for their propaganda value.

But the modern urge to categorize has roots that go even further back, to scientific and rational Enlightenment practices of encyclopedic documentation and classification. In the realm of the visual arts, the categorical impulse was connected with the accuracy of representation, whether in observations of the natural world or in portraiture. The practice took root in popular culture, notably in the widespread serial depiction of cultural customs, types, and trades, which circulated either in series of cheap prints or in albums of watercolors. Caricature, the exaggeration of physical characteristics for comical, satirical, or political effect, took this interest in observation to the extreme. In the wake of the French Revolution, the country's magazines were filled with the biting visual wit of artists like Charles Philipon, Honoré Daumier, and Paul Gavarni; with the growth of the popular press during the nineteenth century, caricature became an admired profession and an effective strategy for political resistance and social satire around the world. The distortions in caricature are meant to reveal a correspondence between physical appearance and personality; emphasis on a single trait, like a large nose or unusual hairstyle, also made the subject instantly recognizable.

Once the postcard craze was in full swing, most prominent political figures of the time were caricatured in sets and series. Perhaps the leader of the postcard caricature was Orens Denizard. He was one of numerous Beaux Arts–trained artists who decided to try their hand at postcards through the genre of caricature. Since it demanded a certain level of drafts-manship and boasted a storied history, caricature was a respectable way to venture into the new, if suspiciously popular, art form. Denizard went on to create nearly a thousand postcards [164–165]. Most were engravings (some hand-colored) or lithographs; many were issued as limited-edition prints, which the artist personally hand-numbered and offered by subscription. For Denizard, the postcard did not mean the abandonment of his academic roots; rather, it was a "a confined format" that offered him a unique opportunity to revive "the satirical print, in honor of the time of Daumier and Gavarni," as he wrote in October 1902 in an open letter to his collectors.[5] Denizard differentiated his small-scale prints from postcards made with modern processes, such as photography, to indicate that they were works of art rather than popular ephemera.

Nonetheless, he and other French artists led the way in creating satirical postcards of all kinds and levels of quality. Many commented on current world events like the Transvaal (or Boer) War in South Africa, the Boxer Rebellion in China, and the Russo-Japanese War. International interest in such subjects fostered a lively dialogue of satirical imagery among postcard artists around the globe. The resulting repertory of exaggerated features and characteristics defined the representation of the important political figures of the day, in political cartoons in newspapers and magazines as well as on postcards. For example, cards issued by Germany's rivals that depicted Kaiser Wilhelm II embellished his enormous moustache, with its two ends reaching impossibly high [155]. Such representations of Germany's leader circulated for more than a decade, tracing the growth of his rapacious imperial ambitions, his reputation as the world's barbarian during World War I, and his whimpering flight into exile in the Netherlands at the end of the war. Russian cartoonists, in turn, delighted in giving Czar Nicholas's Svengali, Grigory Rasputin, the look of a madman as he manipulated the czar and his wife, Queen Alexandra [166–167]. Repetition made public figures identifiable at a rapid glance, allowing the political message to come through. Such figures,

157 Czar Nicholas II and family in a rowboat, before 1917

Ихъ Императорскія Величества Государь Императоръ и Государыня Императрица, Великія Княжны Ольга и Татіана Николаевны на прогулкѣ въ Финляндскихъ шхерахъ.

especially the royals—longtime symbols of status and style—were the major celebrities of the time, even among less politically inclined citizens.

Postcards of royals signaled a changing world. As Napoleon III had done with the *carte-de-visite*, turn-of-the-century royalty produced official postcards for propaganda purposes with formally staged portraits displaying the requisite royal trappings. But as cracks in monarchical systems began to show, and the traditional European aristocracy lost wealth and political power, their influence on public taste waned. *Harper's Bazaar* noted in 1894 that even fashion had been "set free from the thraldom of the king's favorites" and instead now followed the dictates of European designers.[6] Perhaps sensing this decline, royal families began to issue postcards in which they appeared without their regalia and in casual settings, as if to suggest their own continued relevance as modern citizens [157]. Newer monarchs like England's Edward VII and Germany's Wilhelm II flouted the decorum and restraint of previous royal generations by leading increasingly public lives and associating with the newly moneyed rather than just the nobility. Illustrated postcards echoed this change, inserting monarchs into public spaces where they took part in distinctively popular activities.

In a series by the French illustrator Charles Naillod, for example, monarchs take up the fashionable pastime of bowling. Edward VII cuts an especially casual figure, with jacket off and sleeves rolled up as he strains to lift the heavy ball [173–176]. Another series, by an artist known only as Elym, equates royals with the turn-of-the-century daredevils who thrilled circus and amusement park audiences with gravity-defying bicycle rides on loop-the-loop tracks (usually with an ambulance waiting nearby). The monarchs, however, hardly project a sense of daring, as they take the loop on incongruous vehicles, including a gondola and a hobbyhorse [177–180]. These evocative images rely on established conventions of caricature and on public knowledge of their subjects—Edward VII's enormous stomach and his cigar, for example, representing his lavish lifestyle and inveterate smoking habit. Combining satire and admiration, such cards both delighted antimonarchists, who took pleasure in caricature's leveling power, and reassured loyalists, who could consider them proof of the monarchs' relevance in the modern world.

158 Jan Olieslagers, about 1910 CÉSAR GIRIS

159 Glenn Hammond Curtiss, about 1910 CÉSAR GIRIS

As the allure of royals diminished, new figures, such as the modern athlete, came into the spotlight of celebrity. Sports figures were celebrated for their performances rather than their pedigree. Many of the earliest stars of bicycle racing, boxing, European football, and baseball were from the working class and used sports to escape from small towns or rough urban neighborhoods. Celebrity was one way to achieve social mobility.

Boxing was one of the first sports through which working-class athletes gained national and even international fame. One of the earliest international celebrity boxers was Jack Johnson, the son of former slaves. He became the first African American world heavyweight champion in 1908, after repeatedly being denied the chance to fight for the title against the white champion, Jim Jeffries. Johnson's fame was fed by his controversial public relationships with white women. Postcard images of Johnson's muscular body circulated widely, and his powerful punches became so well known that British soldiers fighting in World War I dubbed certain heavy explosives "Jack Johnsons" because they produced a large amount of black smoke [181–182].

The celebrity type that perhaps best represents the early twentieth century is the aviator. Flying was new, glamorous, and dangerous, and postcard series of these daring pioneers of the sky abounded. Unlike other celebrities known solely for their appearance, aviators were identified with their planes. A common postcard format featured a vignette of the celebrity aviator tucked into the corner of a larger photograph of his plane. Flyers who appeared on cards included the Frenchman Louis Blériot and his series of eponymous aircraft, one of which he used in the first flight across the English Channel, and the U.S. aviator Glenn Curtiss, who with his biplane won some of the first speed competition prizes. Yet there was plenty of room for inventiveness in representations of aviators. A common metaphor identified them with their avian fellow flyers, as shown by the humorous series *Modern-oiseaux* (Modern Birds) [158–159]. Wilbur Wright, the first person to achieve sustained controlled flight, also captured the public imagination because of his perceived resemblance

to a bird. He was even called "the first 'man-bird'" by one of his contemporaries.[7] Caricaturists played on Wright's attributes, exaggerating his beaklike nose, jutting chin, and the bill of his signature cap [188–189].

During the postcard craze, celebrities provided a wealth of material for those who depicted them and those who collected them. There is much more than meets the eye in postcard depictions of celebrities, as they bring together several philosophical and representational strands of the previous centuries. Celebrity postcards are among the best demonstrations of the postcard artist's ability to find yet another way to represent something familiar. Sheer variety was not enough, though. As the British cartoonist Phil May noted in 1906, in their constant search for the new, postcard collectors always "demanded something more subtle and ingenious" than what had come before.[8]   L.K.

1. Charles Simond, "La carte postale," in *Paris de 1800 à 1900: Les centennales parisiennes; panorama de la vie de Paris à travers le XIXe siècle* (Paris: Plon-Nourrit, 1903), 150; Jules Claretie, *La vie à Paris, 1904* (Paris: Bibliothèque-Charpentier, 1905), 102.
2. Frederic T. Corkett, "The Production and Collection of the Pictorial Postcard," *Journal of the Society of Arts* 54 (April 27, 1906): 628.
3. Aldo Maggioni, "La I.ª Esposizione Internazionale di Cartoline Postali Illustrate a Venezia: Note ed appunti," *Emporium* 10 (1899): 310.
4. "National Portraits," *The Times*, April 7, 1932, cited in Aaron Jaffe, *Modernism and the Culture of Celebrity* (Cambridge: Cambridge University Press, 2005), 171.

5. Bruno de Perthuis, "Les estampes politiques sur cartes postales au début du XXe siècle," *Nouvelles de l'estampe* 110 (May–June 1990): 14–25; 19.
6. "Changing Costumes," *Harper's Bazaar* 27, no. 15 (April 14, 1894): 294.
7. Claude Grahame-White, *The Aeroplane: Past, Present, and Future* (Philadelphia: Lippincott, 1911), 3. See also Robert Wohl, *A Passion for Wings: Aviation and the Western Imagination, 1908–1918* (New Haven: Yale University Press, 1994), 5.
8. "Humour by Post, Illustrated Chiefly by Drawings from Phil May," *The Strand Magazine* 32 (September 1906): 180.

160

161

Caricatures of royalty, 1903

GEO (HENRI JULES JEAN GEOFFROY)

160

Leopold II, king of Belgium

161

Edward VII, king of the United Kingdom

162

Theodore Roosevelt, about 1905

P. P.

163

Czar Nicholas II, about 1905

HENRI PIERRE

163

162

164

Prince Potemkin. The torch burns . . . it's over, 1905

ORENS DENIZARD

165

The Russian candle, 1905

ORENS DENIZARD

165

Его величество
Григорій, далеко не Первый, но, къ счастью, послѣдній,
Самодержецъ Всероссійскій.

166

Гришкѣ игрушки, а Россіи слезки.

167

166
Rasputin, about 1912

167
Rasputin, about 1917
W.

168

Roosevelt—Enough! about 1905

TOMÁS JÚLIO LEAL DA CÂMARA

169

Mr. Roosevelt separates the combatants, 1905

MILLE

170

Peace. The position of Mr. Roosevelt, 1905

F. MARMONIER

168

169

170

171

The gas trust, probably 1903

ROSTRO

172

An American millionaire, about 1900

171

172

173

174

Bowling kings, about 1911
CHARLES NAILLOD

173
Bowling in Berlin

174
Bowling in Brussels

175

176

175
Bowling in Saint Petersburg

176
Bowling in London

177

Looping the loop, before 1906
ELYM

177
Edward VII,
king of the United Kingdom

178
Émile Loubet,
president of France

179
Victor Emmanuel III,
king of Italy

180
Wilhelm II,
emperor of Germany

178

179

180

181

182

FAMOUS AND FAMILIAR

181–182

Jack Johnson, about 1910

183–185

She really gets around
(*Mona Lisa!*), about 1913

183

184

185

186

186

Ferdinand, Count Zeppelin, 1909

H. ROTH

187

Zeppelin on a Paris–London joyride, 1914

HANS MÜLLER

188

Wilbur Wright, 1909

H. ROTH

189

Wilbur Wright. Flight, American style, after 1903

MODEL BY CÉSAR GIRIS

187

188

189

POWER, SPEED, AND FLIGHT

I have often attempted to analyse this craving for speed. . . . When I drove a 4 h.p. car, I craved for a 6, and after that the speed obtained from an 8 h.p. engine seemed to offer every bliss in life. From 20 to 30 and from 30 to 40 miles an hour and then on again, and perhaps because I then took to racing, speed pure and simple appealed to me beyond everything else.

— CHARLES JARROTT,
Ten Years of Motors and Motor-Racing, 1906

Imagine a child who came into the world in 1869—the year the postcard itself was born. If she lived to her eightieth birthday and looked around to take stock of that world, she would have found it utterly transformed. In 1869 Thomas Edison's first patent for an incandescent lightbulb was still ten years in the future; the automobile was just the dream of a carriage that would not need a horse; and airplanes were strictly science fiction. Over the next eight decades that child would live through a period of technological ferment without parallel in human history. Electricity came out of the laboratory into the factory and the home. Petroleum conquered the world, becoming essential to everything from fuels to plastics to fertilizers. Airplanes evolved from dream to popular spectacle to means of travel and weapon of war. The automobile spread like a blessing and a plague, and horses disappeared from everyday life. The child of

1869 lived through the creation of moving pictures, talking pictures, radio, and even television.

These technologies wrought great changes in how people perceived and interacted with their world. By releasing the energy stored in oil and gas, machines made superhuman labor possible. Automobiles and planes shrank distances. The blur and fragmentation associated with speed and the dizzying perspective of height helped define the era's visual language. The machines even seemed to change people's sense of time. Writers from Henry Adams in the United States to Robert Musil in Austria noted the world's ever more frenetic pace. Obsessed with statistics, commentators sought to quantify the age's increasingly time-conscious character. The sociologist Georg Simmel, for example, noted an enormous increase in the sale of pocket watches during the 1890s; Fred Corkett, of the publisher Raphael Tuck, cited the speed and brevity of the postcard itself.[1]

Of all the technological changes over those eight decades, electricity presented the greatest paradox. Its effects can be very intimate: it lights a bulb that illuminates a book; it heats an iron that presses our clothes; it drives a fan that dries our hair. But electricity's role in those very private moments requires the existence of an elaborate technological web spun by power companies and utilities. The bulb lights only because of power plants, transformers, transmission lines, seemingly infinite lengths of wire, and count-

less workers who tend every part of the system. To finance the construction of that hugely expensive grid, electrical manufacturers and power companies had to promote their products to consumers in as compelling and personal a way as possible. Their very survival depended on it.

Postcards were perfectly suited to the task, for just as electricity crossed the divide between public and private, so could cards. They delivered messages to one person at a time, but on an industrial scale. Perhaps because of that, postcards on electrical themes almost always promote domestic products. Lightbulbs, for example, the most common and humble electrical object, appear on postcards by the thousands, advertised using every conceivable visual metaphor. Bulbs serve as objects of sunny, domestic devotion or are cast as miraculous objects that dazzle primitive peoples; they hang in the night sky to catch astronomers by surprise and light the way down darkened paths, each globe inscribed with the name of its manufacturer [190, 193–196].

One German card boasts no lightbulb at all. The caption reads simply "Electric Light," as a broom sweeps away the kerosene lamps and lighting appa-

ratus of the pre-electrical age. The back has no space for a personal message, as the company has claimed that spot for itself: "Electric light. Advantageous light; cost per hour (for 25 candlepower), only 1.5 cents. Low-cost installation." Another card, issued around 1910 by the Bureau for the Utilization of Electricity, in Berlin, is even more direct: "Electric light: cheaper than petroleum." The slogan was central to the organization's campaign to persuade consumers that the initial cost of installing electricity would quickly be repaid in lower energy bills. It appeared on a coordinated assault of posters, pamphlets (customized for businesses ranging from metalworking shops to beauty parlors), postcards, collectible stickers, and newsletters—one directed "to the housewife" and another "to the landlord" [197–198].[2]

Cards for other sorts of electrical appliances were usually less imaginative, but the message was much the same: be up-to-date, go electric. The cartoonist Fred Cooper spelled it out in his cards for Westinghouse. Because the earliest electric irons looked exactly like their nonelectric predecessors, the happy housewife on his card is accompanied by a hint: "See the cord? Being a modern housekeeper, she uses a

191 Woman using electrical appliance, about 1936
LAWRENCE STERNE STEVENS

Westinghouse Electric Iron." To make sure that customers could recognize their products in the store, Westinghouse included small photographic images of the appliances on the back of the cards [199–200]. Even as late as the 1930s, when household electricity had become widespread, advertisers still associated it with modern ease. Around 1936 the Belgian trade association for electricity commissioned the young American Lawrence Sterne Stevens to create a series of cards showing women as they make coffee, iron clothes, and blow-dry their hair. The cards are not advertisements for specific products; instead, they sell the idea that electricity itself will make you more beau-

tiful and stylish [191, 201–202]. It seems fitting that after Stevens returned to the United States, he spent much of his career producing pictures of scantily clad women for the covers of science fiction magazines.

Along with electrical power, the end of the nineteenth century brought speed in many forms: faster trains, faster ships, faster mail service. But nothing so perfectly captured the lust for speed as the automobile, for nowhere else were speed and power so directly under one person's control. Automobiles quickly came to be associated with unfettered freedom for drivers and entrepreneurs alike. Before 1900 the automobile was still an "open" technology: there were no rules and no traditions in automotive design, and the market was not yet dominated by large companies. If you had a good idea about how to make a cart or carriage move under its own power, there was little to keep you from building a vehicle that might make your fortune. The result was boundless inventiveness, as designers explored every possible configuration of body and power train. The menagerie of odd-looking cars that speed across Fernand Fernel's postcards look like a fantasy from a children's book, but nearly all of them appeared on real roads [205–208].

As soon as people started making automobiles, drivers began to race them. One early passion was the long-distance road race, in which drivers and striving auto companies entered cars to see which could get from one city to another first. Often the challenge was just to arrive intact. The most famous of these races (and perhaps the inspiration for Fernel's postcards) was slated to run from Paris to Madrid in 1903. After a series of dramatic crashes left several people dead and many of the fantastical cars wrecked, the race was called off in Bordeaux. Even so, the allure of racing endured, and Fernel's cards both captured the excitement of the speeding cars and helped pioneer a visual language of speed. Over and over again, poster and postcard artists mounted a can of gasoline or oil on wheels and sent it streaking down the road, ready to power or lubricate your car. Some of the most dramatic designs, in which motorcycles almost dis-

solve into streaks of color, echo works by the Italian Futurist artists, who celebrated everything new, fast, and disorienting [192, 209–212].

Ultimately, flight became the most pervasive symbol of technological change in the first half of the twentieth century, perhaps because it was also the most novel. As one author put it in 1917, "Flying has been compared to many things; but, in truth, no comparison is good."[3] That did not keep writers from trying to capture the sensation, which would actually be alien to most of today's air travelers as well. The first planes were small and flimsy; they flew very low, where the air is turbulent; and pilots and passengers were exposed to the weather, for until the 1920s most planes had open cockpits. Accounts usually begin with the sensation of flight itself—of how the plane almost swims through the air, plunging through clouds and dodging the weather; but eventually all of the writers turn their attention from the air to the ground, and to the special perspective on the earth that flying provides: "Things look so different that the mind is aroused to speculation on the reality and the justness

of its previous conceptions. Earth, forests, seas, cities, roads and other familiar things are found no longer to fit into the old pigeon-holes. Subconsciously we realize that the world is not cut-and-dried; that there is always another point of view from which to look at it and at life itself."[4]

Such descriptions served a purpose, for while airplanes may have been a popular obsession, flying itself was not yet a common experience. Pilots became celebrities partly because there were relatively few of them, and in the 1900s and 1910s most people experienced flight by watching planes rather than flying in them. Perhaps because of that, postcards that advertise the earliest air shows tend to be firmly rooted on the ground, featuring scenes of people who look up at the planes rather than images from the perspective of flight. A favorite motif is the moment when a group of planes appears on the horizon, descending from the sky like a flock of birds. The juxtaposition of old and new is another common theme; one card, for a 1913 air show at Halberstadt, in central Germany, captures the excitement as the planes come in low over the

town. The aircraft seem to dance with the towers of a thirteenth-century church, as one era's reach for the sky encounters another's [213].

World War I brought enormous improvements to planes, and many more people began to have the experience of flight itself. As early as 1919, passenger air service started between Paris and London (a direct outgrowth of the war, as the first passenger airplanes on the route were based on a design for a heavy bomber). But air travel was still a luxury, and when Dorothy Sayers had her aristocratic detective Lord Peter Wimsey fly from Paris to London in her 1926 novel *Clouds of Witness*, she was making a point about Wimsey's wealth and social status as much as she was about the urgency of his need to get back to England to save his brother from an accusation of murder. Soon, as aircraft became more robust and commercial flights more common, the visual language associated with flight began to shift as well. Cards from the later 1920s and 1930s frequently show planes high in the air, often from the perspective of someone magically suspended in the sky [217].

The most dramatic cards about flight are those from Fascist Italy. Benito Mussolini, who fancied himself a pilot, tied propaganda for his modern imperial Italy to the freedom and power represented by the airplane. During the late 1920s and 1930s, the Fascist government organized great air rallies—faster and more intimidating versions of the earlier air shows. Borrowing from the blurred representations of speed that had characterized earlier postcards as well as from works by the Italian Futurist artists (many of whom became ardent Fascists themselves), the postcards and posters for those events are filled with abstracted planes and aggressive diagonal lines. One of the most dynamic, created for a 1934 air show at Taliedo, outside of Milan, takes the view from above as its subject, with silhouetted planes in the air, the air terminal's roof, and the runway on the ground all locked together in an intricate pattern [223].

The grandest Fascist air shows were the *crociere aeree*, or "air cruises." In the years before 1930, Mussolini's air minister, Italo Balbo, organized great aerial excursions around the Mediterranean—symbolically reclaiming with a modern fleet the body of water the ancient Romans had called simply *mare nostrum*, "our sea." Then, in 1930 and 1931, Balbo led a fleet of seaplanes all the way to Brazil, perhaps as a demonstration of the newfound power and energy of the home country to the large Italian community in South America. That first Atlantic crossing generated such publicity that Balbo and Mussolini immediately began planning for another. The new cruise, even more ambitious, was to mark the tenth anniversary of the Fascist government. Twenty-five enormous seaplanes left Rome on July 1, 1933. They crossed Europe and set out over the Atlantic, with Chicago and its world's fair as the ultimate goal. When the fleet arrived on July 15, tens of thousands of people greeted the planes as they flew in low over Soldiers Field and eventually settled into Lake Michigan near the Century of Progress exhibition [224–225]. Appropriately enough, the Italian pavilion at the fair bore some resemblance to a gigantic airplane. B.W.

1. Stephen Kern, *The Culture of Time and Space, 1880–1918* (Cambridge, Mass.: Harvard University Press, 1983), 109–17.
2. E. Wikander, "Elektricitätspropaganda und sonstige Mittel zur Erhöhung des Absatzes von elektrischen Strom und elektrischen Apparaten," *Elektrotechnik und Maschinenbau: Zeitschrift des Elektrotechnischen Vereines in Wien* 31 (February 2, 1913): 91.
3. Charles Cyril Turner, *The Marvels of Aviation: Describing in Non-technical Language the Beginnings, Growth, and Achievements of All Kinds of Aircraft* (Philadelphia: Lippincott, 1917), 248.
4. L. C. Everard, "Visual Material: Spur or Sedative," *Visual Education: A National Organ of the New Movement in American Education* 1, no. 5 (Sept.–Oct. 1920): 33.

223 (detail)

193

193

A new star: The Métallique, after 1908

STELMANS

194

Bergmann lightbulbs, about 1910

CARL ZANDER

194

195

196

195
Philips Argenta, before 1928
HANS OERTLE

196
Philips lightbulbs, about 1909

197
Electric light. Cheaper than
petroleum, about 1910

198
Electric light, about 1910
MARTIN LEHMANN-STEGLITZ AND
WALTER LEHMANN-STEGLITZ

197

198

The *Aristocrat* of the
Breakfast Table -
The WESTINGHOUSE
Electric Toaster Stove

199

See the cord? Being a modern
housekeeper she uses a
**Westinghouse
Electric Iron**

200

199–200

Westinghouse appliances, after 1914

FREDERICK GOSS COOPER

201

202

201–202
Women using electrical appliances, about 1936
LAWRENCE STERNE STEVENS

203
Electric fan, about 1930
LAWRENCE STERNE STEVENS

204
Marelli fans, about 1930

203

204

205

205–208

Car racing, about 1903

FERNAND FERNEL

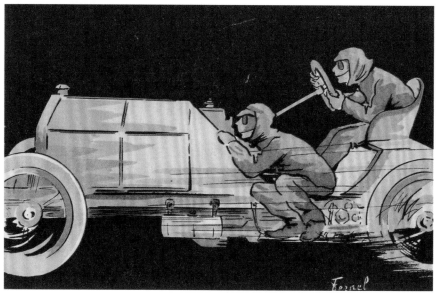

206

207

208

209
Shell. Oil + gas = speed!
about 1930

210
Shell gas and oil, about 1920
A.E.

209

210

211

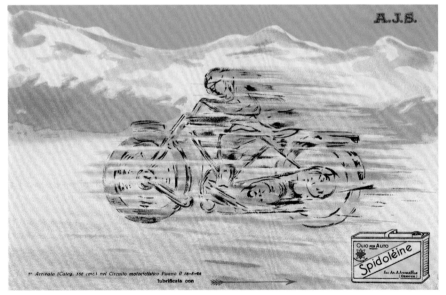

212

211–212
Spidoléine oil, 1924

213

214

213

Flight over the Harz Mountains to Halberstadt, 1911

RICHARD THOMAS

214

Prince Heinrich flight, 1913

ERNST RIESS

215

216

215

East Prussian flight, 1913

H.W.

216

Aeronautical Exposition, New York, 1919

JOHN E. SHERIDAN

217

217
Great Aeronautics Exhibition, 1934

218
The sky, the sea; probably before 1941

219
Air France. Best wishes for 1935, 1934

220
Air Condor. Merry Christmas and
Happy New Year, about 1930

218

219

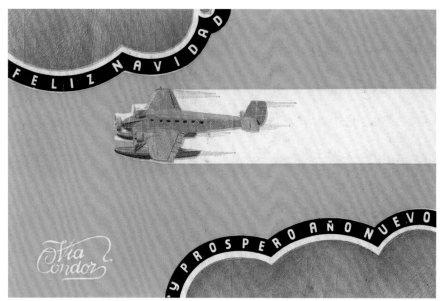

220

221

221
MAK π 100 celebration at the
Italian air academy, about 1930
DE ROBERTIS

222
MAK π 100, about 1930

223
Taliedo. Great aviation day, 1934
N. LONGO (?)

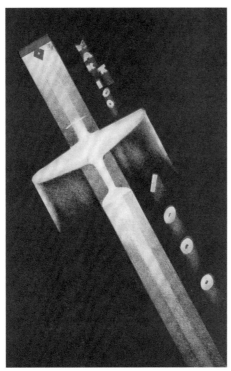

222

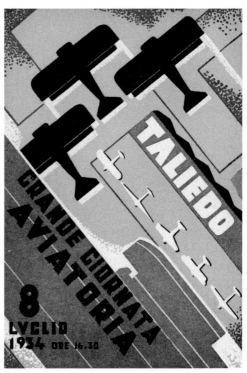

223

224

225

224
Decennial air cruise, 1933
MARCELLO DUDOVICH

225
Decennial air cruise, 1933
LUIGI MARTINATI

226

226

The airship *Graf Zeppelin* uses Veedol motor oil exclusively, about 1931

227

The zeppelin hall at Rhein-Main airport, about 1935

228

The *Hindenburg* disaster, 1937

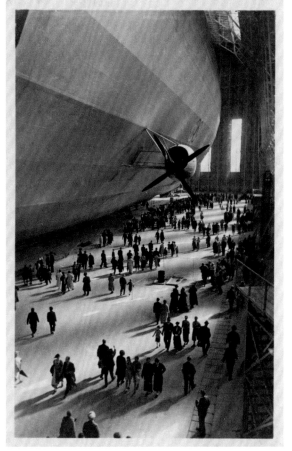

227

228

MAKING THE SALE

Let's go to the café. Would we order a drink without giving a name? On the contrary, most liqueurs and aperitifs are known by their maker . . . one orders, for example, a Pernod.

— JULES ARREN, "Sa majesté, la publicité," 1908

But it is not just Pernod. Arren continues: "A draftsman, in an art supply store, will specify the number and brand of pencils that he wants. In a grocery, a cook will buy some products by weight or volume, without other specification; but if she wants packaged cookies or patés, she will ask for particular brands . . . which come in the manufacturer's own packaging. All this is sufficient to demonstrate that for certain of our needs, we ask for things by adding a name or brand, and for others we do not. This simple fact has infinite consequences for industry and commerce."[1]

These words describe a world that still sounds familiar today. Like the drinker, the artist, or the shopper of the *belle époque*, we order things by brand name, too: Levi's, not jeans; Fritos, not corn chips; Absolut, not vodka. This phenomenon, second nature to us, was novel enough to draw comment at the turn of the last century. Brand awareness arose in a newly commercialized world in which, for the first time, a broad mass of consumers had access to many different versions of essentially the same product. Why did the drinker at the café order Pernod and not some other anise-flavored liqueur? The answer, according

to Arren, was advertising, a force he celebrated in a series of books and articles, two of which bear the magnificent title *His Majesty, Advertising*.

Advertising was nothing new, of course: ancient Roman amphorae bear advertisements for, among other products, *garum*, or fermented fish sauce.[2] But the decades before 1900 were the first to be truly saturated with advertising. By the end of the nineteenth century, cities like Paris and New York were drowning in posters, placards, and signboards, as advertisers fought for attention on billboards, kiosks, and construction fences. The array of words and images could be overwhelming, as posters were slapped over posters in a dazzling collage of images and type [12]. In a time before the advent of mass media like radio and television, there were relatively few ways an advertiser could make a direct appeal to one person at a time—postcards were among them.

Postcards and advertising were married almost from the start, partly because postcards had a direct commercial ancestor—the trade card. Businesses issued these colorful lithographed cards to tempt customers and collectors alike, sometimes selling them but more often just giving them away. In the 1870s and 1880s, people collected trade cards with an ardor similar to that which they brought later to postcards. Much like postcards, trade cards bore advertisements, cartoons, new year's messages, and commentary on the news and events of the day, but because trade cards could not propel themselves

through the post and appear, unbidden, in someone's mailbox, collectors tended to keep trade cards for themselves, pasted into albums. The emergence of postcards changed the rules of the game, for postcard buyers could send them along to their friends, giving the sales pitch extra life at no cost to the advertiser.

Postcards were doubly valuable because they could extend the lifespan of the ephemeral images that appeared on posters. Around 1900 the British publisher Raphael Tuck had great success with a long run of postcards called "Tuck's Celebrated Posters." The series gave customers a chance to collect designs that were awkward to store in their original format and provided advertisers a means of keeping poster designs in the public eye long after the originals had been covered up or ripped down. The celebrated poster artist Leonetto Cappiello openly declared his love for postcards in 1904, not only because they embodied "communication by image" but also because they provided "a most useful means of disseminating art."[3] Even into the 1920s, many of Cappiello's advertising posters—for Omega watches, Gancia Asti Spumante, or Bitter Campari—led second lives in the smaller format [233–234, 237].

Magazines made extensive use of cards, too, both as advertisements for the journals themselves and as a means of promoting the work of their artists. One long-lasting French postcard series from the 1890s reproduced magazine covers from around the world. In the next decade, the stylish anarchist weekly *L'assiette au beurre* (literally, "the butter plate," meaning something like our "pork barrel") issued postcards that reproduced images from the magazine and even published whole postcard-themed issues.[4] And in Germany, the 1898 edition of a guide to the Alte Pinakothek, Munich's museum of old-master paintings, included an advertisement for the avant-garde art magazine *Jugend* (Youth). The ad offers reprints of images from the publication in the form of playing cards, small posters, and, most prominently, postcards, available singly or in series of twenty-five.[5] The cards were, in effect, advertisements for *Jugend*'s new artistic brand, Jugendstil.

Postcards quickly became part of integrated advertising campaigns. In Milan, the music publisher Ricordi, best known for championing the works of the opera composers Giuseppe Verdi and Giacomo Puccini, branched out into printing other kinds of graphics

233 (detail)

RICORDO
GRANDI MAGAZZ
ITALIANI
&E.A. MELE
NAPOLI

230 Michelin tires, Houston, Texas, about 1910

in the 1890s. The company established the Officine Grafiche Ricordi, a printing office that functioned essentially as an advertising agency. Most of Ricordi's images were unrelated to music, as the company hired some of Italy's most stylish artists, such as Aleardo Villa and Franz Laskoff, to craft the public face of businesses as varied as Talmone chocolate and the Mele department stores [235–239]. While Ricordi became famous for its posters, the company took advantage of its presses and artists to produce catalogues, newsletters, and postcards as well. Images moved fluidly from one medium to another, and it can be difficult to determine whether a particular illustration began life as a catalogue cover, a poster, or a postcard.[6]

The relationship between Ricordi and the Mele chain, based in Naples, was especially fruitful. Year after year, Ricordi's artists produced posters that garnered appreciative notices in the local press, which noted the quality of the posters themselves, praising their "beauty of line" and "efficacy of color," as well as the "impeccable precision" of the printing. Such reports usually coincided with the sudden appearance of new posters around town and often included free advertising in the form of detailed descriptions of the clothing they showed. The posters that were

"so 'chic,' so rich, so Parisian!" must have seemed like magical windows onto a more cosmopolitan world. In 1897, one writer seems almost to have fallen in love with a woman in such a poster: "Here is a beautiful woman of confident bearing. Having made her exquisite *toilette*, on a beautiful autumn or winter day, and warm under her fur mantle, in a handsome outfit of the color beige with a most fanciful hat arrayed atop her blonde hair and holding a bouquet of fresh flowers . . ." Clearly, the posters were effective advertising. But they were also large—sometimes so large that the originals came in several pieces—so Mele and Ricordi issued postcards as well. The publishers took care to preserve the posters' aura of worldly sophistication and the high quality of the printing, while providing seductive images in a format that was a bit more convenient for the aspiring consumer.[7]

The most inventive firms, such as the French tire company Michelin, created completely integrated brand identities. Beginning in the 1890s, the company adopted Bibendum, the animate stack of tires better known today as the Michelin man, as its sole mascot. (He is white because the earliest rubber tires were white, not black.) Bibendum's name comes from a line in the *Odes* of the ancient Roman poet Horace

231–232 Falstaff beer, about 1909

that reads "Nunc est bibendum"—loosely, "Now's the time for a drink." The idea was that the inherent strength and durability of Michelin tires guaranteed that nothing so irritating as a flat would get in the way of the real purpose of cycling and motoring, namely, enjoying oneself.

Bibendum was everywhere Michelin was found. He appeared on postcards and posters, graced the company's travel and dining guides, and even took three-dimensional form.[8] The campaign was fully international. On one card, a Dutch Bibendum sets out to conquer the roads that lead out of Holland;

he even includes a personal "handwritten" message on the back, reminding his friends—"Amice!"—that Michelin bicycle tires are the best and fastest. In Houston, Texas, a pair of giant Bibenda sit atop a truck, two North American members of a family of inflatable Michelin men who paid visits to fairs and carnivals throughout the world. And, from a charming series of Italian cards, a very suave Bibendum sips champagne (perhaps from the bottle labeled "Elixir of Glory") and smokes a cigar. He's deep in conversation with Caesar and Napoleon, who warn him to watch out for his Brutus or his Waterloo. "Pah! It's nothing to me," he responds, "my papa Michelin made me invincible and invulnerable" [230, 240–241].

Advertising postcards are a sensitive barometer of the ideas companies thought would resonate with customers. In the 1890s, for example, firms that made rubber tires repeatedly depicted women cyclists on their postcards, a reminder of the independence of action and freedom to flirt that a bicycle could provide [242–244]. Brewers, by contrast, clearly aimed at male consumers, as the smiling barmaids who peek around bottles of Falstaff beer make clear [231–232]. Advertisers also quickly adopted the art of anthropomorphism. In the 1920s, *La sartotecnica*, an Italian catalogue for tailors, advertised itself with a very confident and well-dressed fellow leaning on a pair of scissors; and food products provided endless inspiration, as a myriad of animate cheeses, fish, and other edibles happily offered themselves up for consumption [245–248].

It is testimony to the central role of advertising in the development of the postcard that advertising cards are found throughout this book. Whatever other stories they may tell, many of the cards for cafés and air shows and roller rinks are also selling things. Even what may be (to art historians, at least) the most recognizable of postcards have a double essence. Those cards, issued by Germany's Bauhaus school of design on the occasion of a 1923 exhibition, celebrated the new artistic world being created at the school [260–263]. A different artist designed each card, providing a quick overview of the many styles that flourished at the Bauhaus. These postcards are often among the very few held by art museums, for to the art world the cards are prints that have, by parentage—Wassily Kandinsky, Paul Klee, László Moholy-Nagy—earned their place in a temple of the Muses. But they are also postcards. And they are also advertisements.   B.W.

1. Jules Arren, "Sa majesté, la publicité," *Le correspondant* 233 (1908): 997–98.
2. R. I. Curtis, "Product Identification and Advertising on Roman Commercial Amphorae," *Ancient Society* 15–17 (1984–86): 209–228.
3. "Numéro spécial: La carte postale illustrée," *Le Figaro illustrée* 175, October 1904.
4. For example, the issue "En cinq-sec, album de cartes postales et revue de l'année, par Crésus," *L'assiette au beurre* 458 (January 8, 1910).
5. Richard Muther, *Der Cicerone in der Münchner Alten Pinakothek*, 5th ed., (Munich: Georg Hirth, 1898), p. 57 of advertising supplement ("Georg Hirth's Publikationen") bound in the back.
6. Luigi Menegazzi, *Il manifesti italiano* (Milan: Electa, 1995), 32–35; Bevis Hiller, *Posters* (London: Spring Books, 1969), 214–21.
7. Mariantonietta Picone Petrusa, *I manifesti Mele: Immagini aristocratiche della "belle époque" per un pubblico di Grandi Magazzini*, exh. cat. (Milan: Mondadori, 1988), 214–31.
8. Stephen L. Harp, *Marketing Michelin: Advertising and Cultural Identity in Twentieth-Century France* (Baltimore: Johns Hopkins University Press, 2001), 1–3, 15–53; Olivier Darmon, *Michelin Man: 100 Years of Bibendum*, trans. Bernard Besserglik (London: Conran Octopus, 1998), esp. 49–54.

233

233

Gancia Asti Spumante, 1922

LEONETTO CAPPIELLO

234

Omega watches, about 1920

LEONETTO CAPPIELLO

234

235

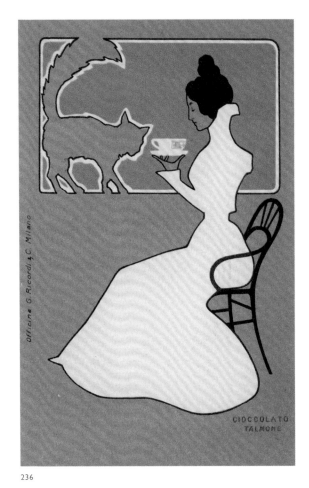

236

235–236

Talmone chocolate, about 1901

FRANZ LASKOFF

237

237–239

Mele department stores, about 1900

POSSIBLY ALEARDO VILLA

239

238

240

Michelin tires, about 1908

CARLO BISCARETTI

241

Michelin tires, about 1910

WINTERS

240

241

242–244

Continental Pneumatic, about 1900

SOME SIGNED G.L.

242

243

244

245

246

245

La Sartotecnica, about 1931

FEDERICO SENECA

246

Danois cheese, about 1930

T. RAYEZ

247

Campari bitters, 1921

LEONETTO CAPPIELLO

248

Albo preserves are the best,
about 1930

248

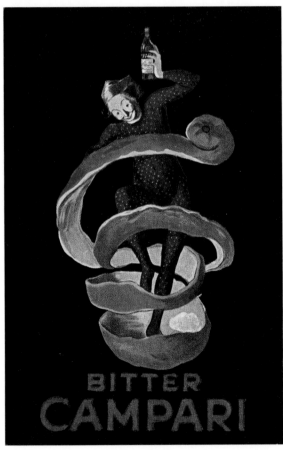

247

249

250

249–252
Rochefort wallpapers, about 1925

251

252

253

253
Carpano vermouth, about 1930?

254
Borsalino hats, about 1936

254

255

256

255–256

Madeleine Vionnet's fashion house, 1922

THAYAHT (ERNESTO MICHAHELLES)

257

257–259
Paul Beyer Graphic Arts, about 1930

Bis heute Hörte ich nichts von Ihnen auf mein Angebot. Darf ich um Ihre Stellungnahme bitten.

Mit Hochachtung!

GRAPHISCHE KUNSTANSTALT
PAUL BEYER

PAUL BEYER GRAPHISCHE KUNSTAN—STALTEN ERFURT ZWEIGGESCHÄFT ZELLA-MEHLIS IN THÜR.

259

Sie werden mit meinen Entwürfen und Klischees zufrieden sein.

GRAPHISCHE KUNSTANSTALT
PAUL BEYER

ERFURT POSTSCHLIESSFACH 221 FERNRUF 2734

PAUL BEYER GRAPHISCHE KUNSTANSTALTEN ERFURT ZWEIGGESCHÄFT ZELLA-MEHLIS IN THÜR.

258

199

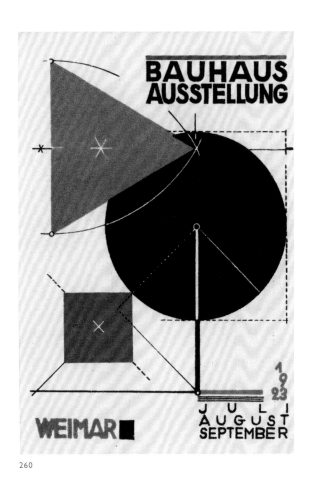

260

261

263

Bauhaus exhibition, 1923

260
Herbert Bayer

261
Wassily Kandinsky

262
Rudolf Baschant

263
Kurt Schmidt

262

Rugby.

HEALTHY BODIES

The status of a country among the nations depends to a very great extent on the system of physical training in vogue. In a nation physical prowess co-exists with mental and intellectual vigor.

—*Eugen Sandow's Magazine of Physical Culture,*1899

In 1897 Eugen Sandow of Prussia, one of the world's first bodybuilders, published the book *Strength and How to Obtain It*, in response to the hundreds of letters he received every day that asked: "Can I become strong?"[1] Sandow's fame originated in feats of strength performed in circuses and music halls throughout Europe, and then spread through appearances on the stages of London and New York, in Thomas Edison's earliest Kinetoscope films, and as a star of Ziegfeld's Trocadero vaudeville. The bodybuilder's amazing powers earned him distinction as "the strongest man in the world." Sandow astounded audiences by lifting enormous amounts of weight, such as that of two men or three small horses and even a pianoforte with an orchestra of eight performers standing on it. He encouraged his admirers to follow his example by describing his own transformation from childhood weakling into virile strongman. Followers sent him charts of their measurements that confirmed his method's effectiveness, accompanied by photographs of their newly muscular bodies. In turn, Sandow sponsored bodybuilding contests, opened a chain of schools, and preached to thousands through

his popular *Magazine of Physical Culture*. In 1911 King George V of England named him the Royal Professor of Scientific and Physical Culture (or the king's personal trainer, in today's parlance).

The British monarch and Sandow's many fans were but a few among many swept up in a wider turn-of-the-century physical culture and sport mania that coincided with the postcard craze. The active body became a frequent topic for postcard artists, spreading the idealized image of the fit modern citizen. Postcards promoted sports organizations' clubs and events and sometimes even served as membership cards. Both the postcards and the athletic body they depicted represented the dynamic twentieth century.

Sports had become a means to build nationalist and patriotic spirit in the late nineteenth century. For example, the Deutscher Schulverein (German School Association), founded in Vienna in 1880, trained members in athletics as part of its goal to preserve Germanic heritage. To propagate its ideas, the organization became a major poster and postcard publisher. A series of cards by Koloman Moser that it issued around 1905 depicts young male gymnasts and makes a potent statement about discipline and fortitude as signs of the abiding strength of German tradition [264–265]. In France, by contrast, athletic development was promoted to counter the physical and symbolic losses experienced during the Franco-Prussian War of the early 1870s. Government encouragement of exercise was part of a larger

effort to create healthier citizens, foster family unity, and repopulate the nation.

The fit figure suggested physical and moral self-control, while its opposite—the physically infirm body—became a sign of character weakness and self-indulgence. During the nineteenth century, the practice of gymnastics, calisthenics, and track and field was added to a number of institutions' activities. Led by schools in Britain and the United States, athletics became part of the curriculum, as a way to build character and patriotism among a nation's future leaders. Sport was also widely employed to instill discipline on military bases or in prisons or prisoner-of-war encampments, as shown in a postcard of a baseball team from the Nebraska state prison [266].

Outside these institutions, numerous European exercise gurus put forward methods to encourage the wider practice of sports. Each promoted a particular fitness ideology. For example, the Frenchman Edmond Desbonnet, one of Europe's most influential proponents of physical culture, attracted the Parisian elite to expensive fitness centers with the latest exercise machines, endorsing personal fitness as a way to combat the decadent lifestyle of the *belle époque*. Sandow's program, which mandated the number and types of weightlifting movements according to age and weight and was designed for men only, promised to produce a universal Greco-Roman body type. In contrast, the Hungarian aristocrat Rudolf von Laban's dance-based system of *Bewegungschöre* (movement chorus), intended for both men and women, stressed free movement and improvisation. Along with new

Opposite:
264–265 Gymnasts, about
1910 KOLOMAN MOSER

266 Nebraska state prison
Black Diamonds

models of physical fitness, long-established exercise philosophies were reconsidered. Per Hendrik Ling's influential Swedish Gymnastics system, developed for military training, continued to attract practitioners even a century after his death, in 1839.

Exercise programs often went beyond the connection between mind and body to connect the human being and nature. The *Lebensreform*, or Life Reform, movement, active in Germany and Switzerland starting in the 1890s, promoted exercise as part of an overall healthy lifestyle, barring the use of alcohol, drugs, and tobacco in favor of sunlight and fresh air. Outdoor activities, like mountain climbing and hiking, became part of the sports craze as well [273–274]. *Deutscher Sport* (German Sports), an extensive postcard series from the turn of the century, documents the many endeavors, from hunting to rowing, that captivated newly active modern citizens, with strong male and female figures set in profile against various open-air settings [275–278].

In addition to individual exercise, organized sports and team games also gained popularity over the course of the nineteenth century. British and U.S. universities again sparked the interest, instituting intercollegiate

competition in track and field, rugby, and baseball. Such contests created spirited rivalries and built allegiances.[2] The lively competition among Ivy League colleges resulted in some of the most inventive and popular early U.S. postcards [19, 44–46]. The emergence of relatively new sports, like skiing, croquet, cricket, and competitive swimming, or those tied to technological improvements and inventions, like skating, bicycling, and auto racing, widened the appeal of athletics for both participants and spectators. By the turn of the century, amateur sports clubs were everywhere. One, the Berliner Sport-Club, formed in 1899 when two earlier student groups merged, remains in existence today. In this club, as in the sports craze in general, social classes remained separated from one another.[3] Games requiring equipment or dedicated spaces, like lawn tennis and golf, were reserved mostly for the aristocratic and leisure classes.

Nonetheless, increased urbanization brought workers into closer contact with the privileged. Labor reform, which gave the working class more leisure time for activities like sports, increased the opportunities for these interactions. The history of bicycling reveals the anxieties around these changing social

205

267–268 Continental Pneumatic, about 1900

relationships.[4] Because bicycles were very expensive at first, cycling was a sport for the moneyed. But popularity and technological advances brought lower prices. The leisure class increasingly came into contact with working-class cyclists—laborers or clerks out for recreation as well as messengers or deliverymen. Class distinctions manifested in the types of exercise, clothing, and even the position one maintained on a bike, differences that provided fodder for a rich crop of postcards. Those who had plenty of time for recreation went on leisurely excursions, dressed to the nines, and rode in elegant upright positions [267]. Those who needed to make better time crouched to gain speed, perhaps dressed in simple wind-resistant caps and tight-fitting jerseys and knickers. Many of the best racers came from the working classes; they were among the first sportsmen to gain celebrity and make a living from prize money or corporate sponsorship. A postcard in which a gaggle of proper ladies turns away from attentions paid to them by a biking team speeding past reveals this new clash of classes [268].

Sports also increased interaction between the sexes, and it is not surprising that discussions of athletics reveal anxieties about the changes in gender roles that were taking place at the time. For men, the cultivation of the perfect body often went hand in hand with a classical ideal of the "perfect man."

Male health and beauty, embodied in rippling muscles, signified masculinity and virility. Sandow's books promoted poses reminiscent of the Greco-Roman sculptures that he claimed had inspired him to become a bodybuilder. Desbonnet's book, *Les rois de la force* (Kings of Strength), equated modern-day strongmen (with colorful monikers such as Ronco, the Saxon Trio, and Apollon) with ancient heroes like Hercules and Theseus.[5]

Women's models were more complicated. Historically, female athletes typically had come from opposite ends of the social scale, either peasant girls and prostitutes or the wealthiest ladies of leisure. But as the nineteenth century progressed, athletics became an integral part of more women's experience, again led by colleges in Britain and the United States. By 1901, the men's professional tennis player Jahial Parmly Paret could declare in *The Woman's Book of Sports* that "the American young woman of the twentieth century counts outdoor sports as much among her accomplishments as she does French or higher mathematics."[6] The growing participation of women in sports raised concerns about the seeming contradiction between femininity and athleticism. A pioneering medical doctor and ardent antifeminist named Arabella Kenealy asserted in 1899, "one cannot possess all of the delicately evolved qualities of

269–270 Continental lawn-tennis balls, about 1900

women together with the muscular and mental energies of man," and added that when a woman participated in sports, she "debased her womanhood, becoming a neuter."[7] Even supporters of women's participation in sports, like Paret, urged moderation and the avoidance of strenuous tests of endurance or athletic pursuits that were "too severe for the feminine physique."[8] More advisable were ladies' sports like golfing, lawn tennis, skating, and field hockey. A postcard series from 1910 by the Austrian Mela Koehler provides a model view of the modern female athlete: slender and stylishly outfitted, she manages to swing a racket, club, or stick with no risk of mussing her carefully constructed ensemble [283–286].

Nonetheless, sports turned out to be one of the women's movement's best allies. The earliest feminists, like Amelia Bloomer—for whom the piece of clothing that became most identified with female athleticism was named—embraced the physical freedom brought by athletic activities. Alice Paul, who in 1917 founded the National Woman's Party in the United States, had starred in basketball while at Swarthmore College.

The contradictory pull between modernity and tradition that characterized the women's movement is evident in the development of sportswear. Adjustments made to women's clothing for freedom of movement in athletics, like shorter skirts, looser sleeves, shirtwaist dresses, and the split skirt, eventually became acceptable in mainstream fashion. But early sportswear consistently attempted to maintain the delicate balance between decorum and practicality. And as long as marriage still provided women's main social role, coed sports could bring new opportunities for courting, as a set of postcards advertising rubber tennis balls suggests [269–270]. Even in sportswear, the feminine coquetry of fashion could not be abandoned.

Once again the sport of bicycling can reveal tensions created by new social roles. Offering increased mobility as well as new occasions for contact between the sexes, bicycling did "more to emancipate women than anything else in the world," as the suffragist Susan B. Anthony famously declared in 1896. She continued, "I stand and rejoice every time I see a woman ride by on a wheel. It gives woman a feeling of freedom and self-reliance. It makes her feel as if she were independent."[9] Many postcards make the connection between the bicycle and women's emancipation. Free to zip around the countryside as never before, she had ample opportunity for new experiences, from drinking and smoking to taking up another distinctly modern hobby, photography, as another set of advertising cards illustrates [137–139]. Yet women in France, for example, could be arrested for wearing split skirts when not accompanied by a bike. And many commentators warned of the danger to a woman's virtue from the act of straddling a bar in public, or potentially to her reproductive capacity from excessively fast or long rides.

But by this time, there was no turning back from the sports craze. The image of the fit and healthy citizen gained in political currency as the vigor of nations was increasingly put on display in collective events or tested in international competitions. For example, the dedication of Hannover's new city hall in 1913 included a sports festival, meant as proof of the vitality of the German populace to Kaiser Wilhelm II, who attended the celebrations [279–280]. As the *fin de siècle* ushered in modern nationalism—exacerbated by World War I—displays of organized sport became routine. By the 1920s, athletic youths were trotted out in national spectacles across the world, whether wearing black shirts in Mussolini's Fascist Rome or the garb of revolutionary soldiers in Mexico City.

The creation of the modern-day Olympic Games by Baron Pierre de Coubertin in 1896 had directly linked national pride to athletic competition. Small spectacles at first, the games did not flourish until the 1920s. A series of postcards from the 1924 Paris Olympics conveys the now familiar modern-day spirit of the games, which hovers between tradition and the cutting edge. It highlights sports with long histories (wrestling and track and field), along with those representative of the modern sports craze (tennis and boxing) [287–290]. The stylized bodies reinforce the association of the classicized body with strength and national unity. But the figures, silhouetted against flat backgrounds and framed with decorative borders, also embody the art deco modernism of the roaring twenties.

Other sets from the period use the rhetoric of the healthy body for explicitly political purposes. For example, Gustav Klucis created a famous series of nine photomontage postcards for the Spartakiada, a national sports competition first held in Moscow in August 1928 that was meant to rival the Olympics. Klucis juxtaposed cut-and-pasted photographic images of athletes with propagandistic slogans, organizational acronyms, and the flat, colored, geometrized planes of Constructivist art to showcase the vigor of a dynamic socialist utopia [295–298]. A decade later, Ludwig Hohlwein's Aryan athletes echo the images from Leni Riefenstahl's *Olympia*, a filmed chronicle of the 1936 games held in Berlin [301–302]. They suggest a national strength and ideal of an entirely different sort, and represent an extreme rhetorical connection between sport and state. The Nazis were certainly not the first or the last to use images of the strong and vital athletic body to represent the character of a nation and the collective superiority of its people. Jesse Owens's record-breaking performance in Berlin, however, offered at least one striking rebuttal.   L.K.

1. Eugen Sandow, "Introduction," *Strength and How to Obtain It* (London: Gale & Polden, 1897).
2. See Richard D. Mandell, *Sport: A Cultural History* (New York: Columbia University Press, 1984), esp. chaps. 7–9.
3. Ralf Schäfer, *Militarismus, Nationalismus, Antisemitismus: Carl Diem und die Politisierung des bürgerlichen Sports im Kaiserreich* (Berlin: Metropol, 2010), 241.
4. See Christopher S. Thomson, "Bicycling, Class, and the Politics of Leisure in Belle Epoque France," in *Histories of Leisure*, ed. Rudy Koshar (Oxford: Berg, 2002), 131–46.
5. Professeur [Edmond] Desbonnet, *Les rois de la force depuis les temps anciens jusqu'à nos jours: Avec 733 photographies et dessins* (Paris: Berger-Levrault/Librerie Athlétique, 1911).
6. Jahial Parmly Paret, *The Woman's Book of Sports: A Practical Guide to Physical Development and Outdoor Recreation* (New York: Appleton, 1901), 1.
7. Arabella Kenealy, "Woman as Athlete," *The Nineteenth Century* 45, no. 266 (April 1899): 644; 641.
8. Paret, *The Woman's Book of Sports*, 89.
9. Susan B. Anthony, quoted in Nellie Bly, "Champion of Her Sex," *New York World*, February 2, 1896, 10.

271
House of David baseball team,
about 1915

272
Sistersville Blues baseball club,
1910

271

272

273

Traversée d'une Crevasse

3634 EDITION PHOTOGLOB CO. ZÜRICH

273

Crossing a crevasse, about 1900

274

Skiing in Switzerland, about 1906

WALTHER KOCH

Wintersport im Kanton Graubünden (Schweiz)
No. 1 Ski

WALTHER KOCH

274

275

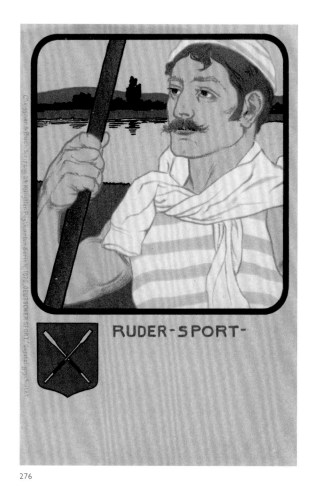

276

German Sports, about 1900

275
Hunting

276
Rowing

277–278
Touring

277

278

279

280

279–280

Hannover sport and festival week, 1913

281

Diana cigarettes, about 1921

ARANKA GYŐRI

282

Berlin Sports Club, about 1925

LUDWIG HOHLWEIN

282

281

283

284

283–284
Women in sportswear, about 1910
MELA KOEHLER

285–286
Continental lawn-tennis balls, about 1900

285

286

217

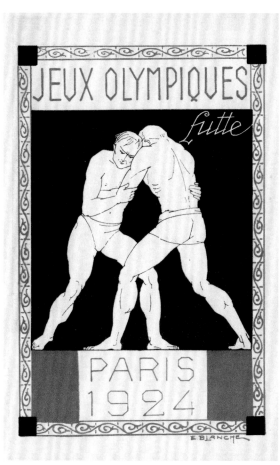

287

288

287–290

Olympic Games, Paris, 1924

E. BLANCHE

289

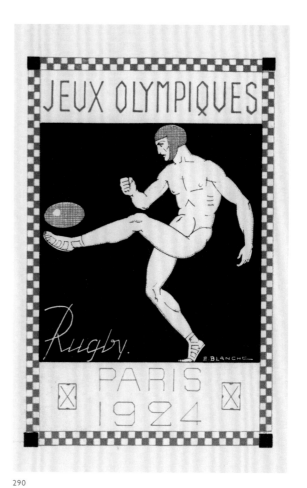

290

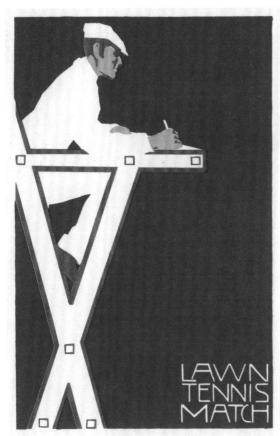

291

291
Lawn-tennis match, about 1930?

292
Football sweepstakes, about 1930?

292

293

294

293–294

Olympic Games, Paris, 1924

H. L. ROOWY

295

295–298

RSI Spartakiada, Moscow, 1928

GUSTAVS KLUCIS

296

297

298

223

299

300

299–300
Third Intercollegiate Games,
Prague, 1932
JIŘI TAUFER

301

302

303

301
Deutsche Lufthansa, 1936
LUDWIG HOHLWEIN

302
Fourth Winter Olympics,
Garmisch-Partenkirchen, 1936
LUDWIG HOHLWEIN

303
The first gold medal for
Germany, award ceremony,
1936

AROUND THE WORLD

To be honest, I don't travel much, and this is why the thought of travel fills me with such longing.

— ROBERT WALSER,
"Something about the Railway," 1907

On July 23, 1803, the South Carolina farmer and politician Francis Kinloch boarded the *John and Francis* and set sail from Charleston, bound for Bordeaux. The little ship, probably less than a hundred feet long and with a crew of fewer than twenty, did not make landfall until September 3. The last two weeks of the voyage were constant frustration. When France was almost within reach, the wind died and then blew in the wrong direction for days. The Napoleonic wars had made the seas unsafe, so the passengers feared they were about to be captured by privateers or detained by the British navy. Worse, the *John and Francis* was near enough to the coast that nighttime became a torment of distant lights—was that flicker on the horizon a star or a lighthouse? When the ship did finally reach France, the port officials held it in quarantine for four days, as there were rumors of horrible diseases coming from the Americas.[1] And yet, maddening though the journey may have been, it was not unusual: peril, discomfort, and delay were the price of going to Europe.

The next century brought changes unimaginable to Kinloch and his fellow passengers. In April 1908 Britain's Cunard Line published its summer schedule of transatlantic crossings. Its four biggest ships would be in regular service from New York to Southampton, with departures in each direction every Sunday and Wednesday.[2] Two of the ships, the *Mauretania* and *Lusitania*, were the largest and fastest liners on the Atlantic, stretching 790 feet (241 meters) from stem to stern. Each could neatly have stored the *John and Francis* crossways at midships. The liners carried more than two thousand passengers and provided the pleasures and amusements of the big city, including fancy restaurants, swimming pools, gymnasia, and top-flight entertainment. Most important, though, they made the ocean crossing in about four-and-a-half days [310–311].

The great ocean liners have come to represent the glamour of travel a century ago, but it was the last two hours of that transatlantic journey that really provide the key to the nineteenth century's great revolution in travel. When eastbound passengers arrived in England, a train came directly to the pier and delivered everyone to central London in just a couple of hours. It was the rail networks—as intricately constructed and carefully calibrated as watches—that permanently shifted the way people experienced time and distance. The before-and-after comparisons for land travel are even more dramatic than those for the sea. In 1819 the journey from Paris to Lyon (about 327 miles) required the better part of a week and some sixty changes of horses; in 1900 it was seven and a half hours by direct train.[3]

304 Oneglia. Sasso olive oils, about 1900

305 Nederland Royal Mail Line, about 1929

By the turn of the century more people were traveling, for business and leisure, than ever before in world history. Postcards helped encourage them, most of all by circulating tempting images of famous buildings and beautiful beaches. The charms of these view cards were irresistible. Long before Walter Benjamin became a philosopher and scholar, he was a boy in turn-of-the-century Berlin, whose desire to roam was spurred by the postcards his grandmother sent from her travels: "I gazed, unable to tear myself away, at the wooded slopes of Tabarz covered with glowing red berries, the yellow-and-white-daubed quays at Brindisi, the cupolas of Madonna di Campiglio printed bluish on blue, and the bows of the *Westerland* slic-

ing high through the waves."[4] Receiving a picture of Rome or Florence or even Skegness in the mail was a powerful spur to dreams of travel.

In the early nineteenth century, leisure travel had been the province of the rich. Most early European resorts—places like England's Bath, Belgium's Spa, and Germany's Baden (Baths)—grew up around sites where mineral springs prized for their medicinal powers bubbled out of the ground. Such destinations remained glamorous and expensive, but as the century progressed, increasing prosperity brought vacation travel within reach of a wider public. For a time, the link between vacations and health remained strong, and people fled cities in the summer, flocking

306 Skegness, about 1908 JOHN HASSALL

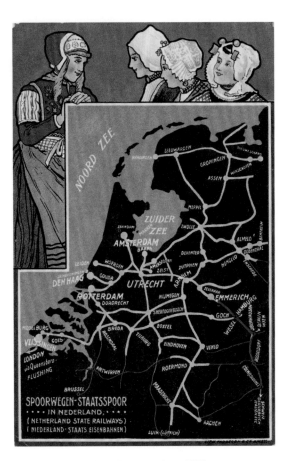

307 Netherlands State Railways, about 1900

to the mountains and especially the seaside, partly from a belief in the healthfulness of sea air. The railways made the process easy, enticing customers with vacation specials, pamphlets, and postcards demonstrating that you could escape to the coast in just a few short hours. Hotels did their part, too, with cards that showed seaside pleasures on the front and listed room rates on the back [314–315].

In Britain and Belgium alike, long stretches of the North Sea coast were converted into resorts.[5] A bank clerk from Brussels might not have been able to afford the spa at Baden, but the coast was a convenient and inexpensive excursion, just an hour and a half from the city. Such North Sea vacations were not rustic

idylls. The resorts were small cities that offered a full complement of urban pleasures. After all, even in high summer the North Sea coast can be harsh and cold, and on those (frequent) summer days when the weather did not cooperate at the beach, holiday towns provided other distractions: racing, tennis, golf, gambling, cafés, and concerts. Ultimately, though, the ocean was the focus, and one of the key rituals at a North Sea resort was to have your picture taken in the water [316–318]. The many postcards of bathers at Ostend led one journalist in 1912 to note acidly that "the real diversion of the bath is the camera."[6]

As the link between vacations and health weakened, resorts were left to rely for their appeal on

308–309 Menu postcards for the Red Star Line, 1905

factors like the quality of their social life. Destinations went in and out of style, and competition could be intense. Was a place exciting, up-to-date, romantic? Did it attract the right sort of people? At a time when much of Europe was still ruled by kings and queens, a royal visitor could make a big difference. Ostend managed to stay at the top of the food chain of North Sea resorts for many decades partly because the kings of Belgium visited regularly. And in 1908 the Spanish city of Santander, in competition with the more fashionable San Sebastián, down the coast, offered to build King Alfonso XIII a new palace. He accepted and afterward visited every summer, helping confirm Santander's place on the social circuit.[7]

Postcards capture each destination's fantasy of itself: a night on a moonlit balcony, a romantic view of a historic site, fun in the sun, or a bracing walk on the beach. But tourism is a cutthroat business, and even as cities and regions promoted their brands, they tried to break into new markets or seasons. In the 1850s, the French Riviera had begun to make a name for itself as a winter resort, but in the 1920s the hotel owners of Nice banded together to promote the city as a summer destination. Their advertising campaign featured an exuberant beachgoer in a floppy hat: "Nice in the summer. What a great vacation!" Newer destinations in Latin America and Asia played up their alluring exoticism for European visitors. In 1934 Rio de Janeiro's tourism office issued a series of cards that featured beautiful women from each European country as a sales pitch for travel to Brazil. The postcards are carefully multilingual, celebrating

Brazil as the "Eterno Paradiso" (eternal paradise), the "Zauber Garten" (magic garden), or, in English, "Epic of Nature." (What exactly the girls have to do with the slogans is left up to the viewer.) Cuba, taking advantage of its proximity to the United States, reminded tourists who were keen for a bit of adventure but nervous about venturing to foreign parts that a forty-minute air journey from safely Anglophone Key West would bring them to Cuba—foreign, yet familiar [321, 327–330].

Shipping companies competed by using postcards of their liners to evoke the elegant life on board. The cards tempted passengers with depictions of the luxurious settings where they would endure a few days of enforced leisure, as they ate and drank their way across the ocean. On the busiest and most prestigious routes, such as the North Atlantic run, competition was flavored by national as well as commercial rivalry. Indeed, governments subsidized many of the largest liners, with an eye to the ships' usefulness in the event of war. Their owners were very conscious of the liners' roles as national ambassadors; the debut of the French Line's glorious and short-lived *Normandie*, in 1935, was accompanied by a profusion of postcard

books celebrating the ship's sleek lines and elegant public rooms—a reminder that French style could reign supreme, even at times of economic distress and political worry [336–337].

Historical sites and seaside towns could be visited year in and year out, but travelers also sought out more ephemeral pleasures. The great parade of world's fairs that had begun in the nineteenth century continued into the twentieth, interrupted only by World War I. The fairs had always featured a disorderly mix of commercial, political, and nationalist messages. That was never truer than in the 1930s, when the exhibitions began to serve as proxies for the national conflicts that would lead, for the second time, to world war. Once again, postcards can bring big stories down to earth. The striking cards from Italy's Triennale d'Oltremare, a 1940 fair that celebrated Italian colonialism, have a sleekly fascist look, but they are also promotions for the firm that designed the fair's maps and signs. And on the back of a shiny card of the Trylon and Perisphere, icons of the 1939 New York fair, the Manhattan Shirt Company greets you: "Creators of the Shirts of Today welcome you to the World of Tomorrow" [345].   B.W.

1. Francis Kinloch, *Letters from Geneva and France*, 2 vols. (Boston: Wells and Lily, 1819), 1–19.
2. Advertisement for Cunard's "New Semi-Weekly Service," *The Travel Magazine* (April 1908): 302.
3. *Galignani's Traveller's Guide through France* (Paris: Galignani, 1819), 2–3; Karl Baedeker, *South-Eastern France, including Corsica*, 3rd ed. (Leipzig: Karl Baedeker, 1898), 2.
4. Walter Benjamin, *Walter Benjamin: Selected Writings*, vol. 2, part 2, *1931–1934* (Cambridge, Mass.: Harvard University Press, 2005), 621.
5. John Beckerson and John K. Walton, "Selling Air: Marketing the Intangible at British Resorts," in *Histories of Tourism: Representation, Identity, and Conflict*, ed. John K. Walton (Clevedon, U.K., and Buffalo, N.Y.: Channel View Publications, 2005), 55–70.
6. R. H. Russell, "On the Sands at Ostende," *The Metropolitan Magazine* 36 (July 1912): 32–33.
7. Carlos Larrinaga, "A Century of Tourism in Northern Spain: The Development of High-Quality Provision between 1815 and 1914," in Walton, *Histories of Tourism,* 98.

344 (detail)

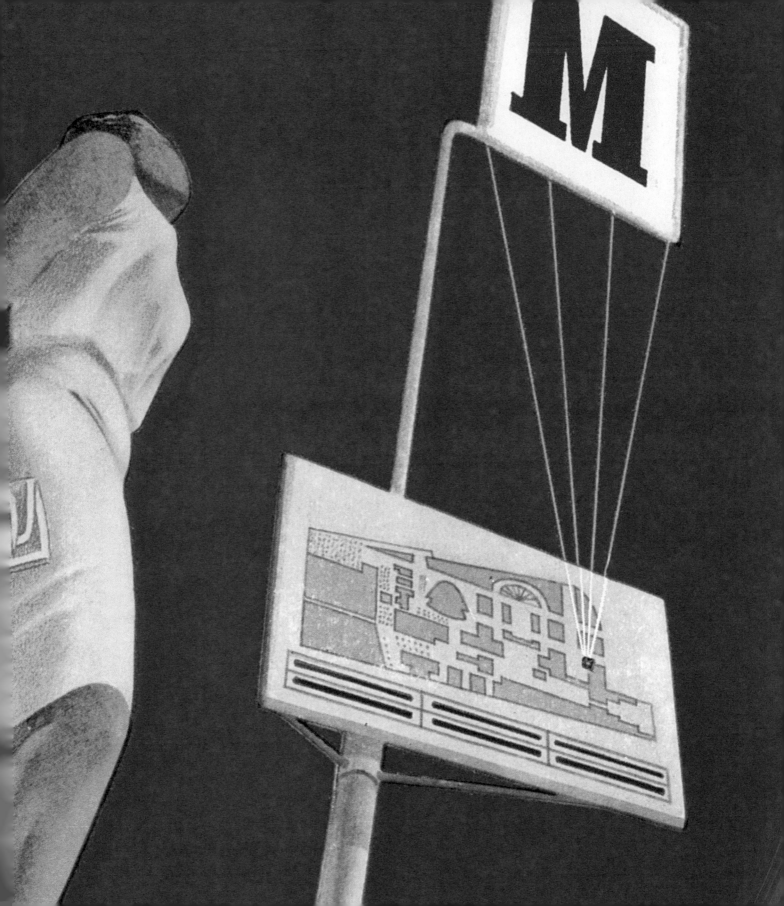

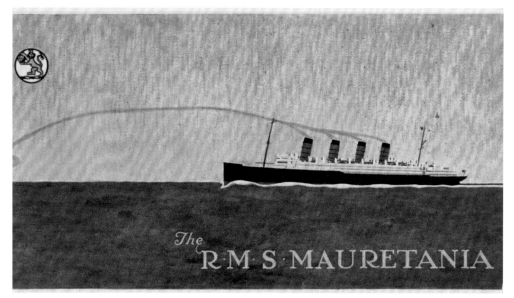

310

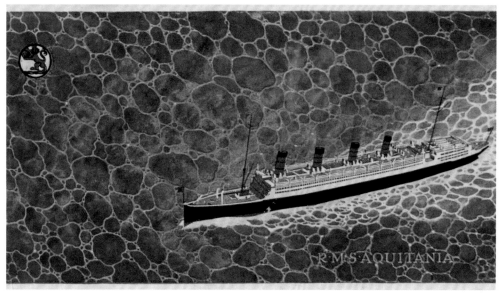

311

310–311
Cunard liners, 1922

The Hamburg–South America
liner *Cap Arcona*, after 1927

312
Sports deck

313
Swimming pool

312

313

314

315

314

Grand Hotel Ocean, about 1900

315

Beach tennis, about 1900

316
Bathing, about 1900

317
Souvenir of Blankenberghe,
Belgium, about 1900

318
Back from bathing, about 1900

316

317

318

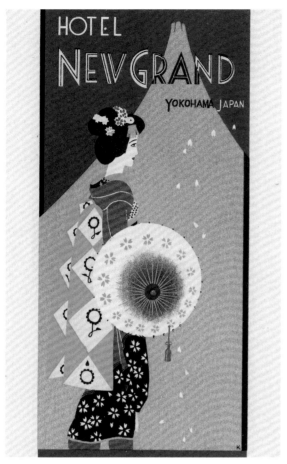

319

320

319–320

Hotel New Grand, Yokohama, Japan,
about 1920

321

Visit Cuba, 1930s?

CONRADO WALTER MASSAGUER

322

Nice in the summer. What a great vacation!
1920s

ER

322

321

323
Riva, on Lake Garda,
about 1900

324
Camogli, Italian Riviera.
Sasso olive oils,
about 1900

323

324

325
Hotel Nettuno, Pisa, about 1910
TOMBI

326
Abbazia, 1936

326

325

327

Rio de Janeiro, 1934
MANUEL MÓRA

327
Magic garden

328
Epic of nature

328

329

329

329
Eternal paradise

330
Flower by the Atlantic

330

331

331
Advance Zephyrs, 1934

332
20th Century Limited, 1938

333
Union Pacific, about 1935

NEW YORK—16 HOURS—CHICAGO, VIA THE WATER LEVEL ROUTE

332

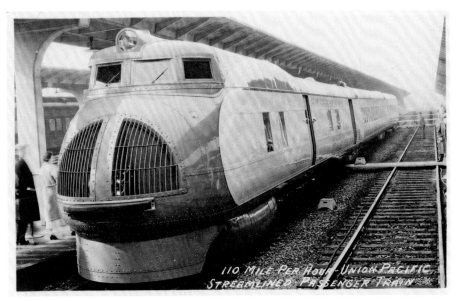

110 MILE PER HOUR—UNION PACIFIC
STREAMLINED PASSENGER TRAIN

333

334

Calmante Rosa motion sickness remedy, about 1935

334
On a train?

335
In a car?

335

336

337

336–337

Postcard booklets of the *Normandie*, 1935–38

338

339

338–341

Valdura products at the Century of Progress
Exposition, Chicago, 1933

340

341

342

343

342–344
Triennial exhibition of the Italian
overseas territories, 1940
CELLA

345
World's Fair, New York, 1939

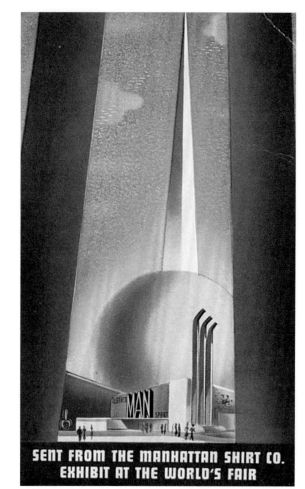

345

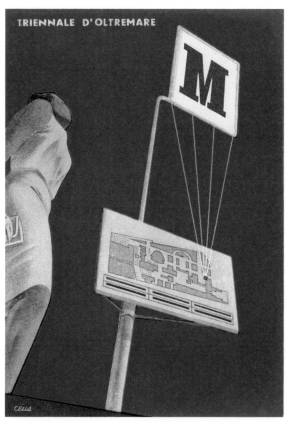

344

THE GREAT WAR

A great quiet reigned everywhere. No bustle no noise, no motor-'buses. Few people in the wide streets, the great Gare St. Lazare, generally so full of English tourists, empty! A Sabbath-like stillness lay over all. . . . One felt that here, indeed, was the echo of the war; that not that many miles away, they, the countless hosts of French and English, were grimly holding the monsters back, fighting the ground inch by inch, and that Paris was looking on, holding her breath, stricken with awe, speechless with the fearful terror of it.

—*The Bystander, August 1914*

By 1914 the world had seen the war coming for more than a decade. It seemed almost beyond imagining that Britain and France and Germany, with their pride and imperial egos, would not eventually slip into conflict. For decades, the great European powers had been able to cooperate on matters like tax treaties, railway gauges, and postal regulations. But they were also economic competitors in a tightly intertwined and industrialized world, as well as the seats of overseas empires. Control of whole continents was at stake, along with fortunes and might on an epic scale. Every empire in world history had been built and sustained by war, and never before had so many empires competed in such close quarters. Yet, when the war did finally come, it caught almost everyone by surprise.

The story needs no detailed retelling. An arms race; a swirling, decade-long diplomatic dance; shifting alliances and rivalries—all pivoting around the crucial poles of Britain and Germany. And, finally, in late June 1914, the assassination of Franz Ferdinand, archduke of Austria. In truth, Austria-Hungary was something of a side player in the whole game, but the Hapsburg empire was so entwined in the jigsaw puzzle of treaties and ententes and alliances that the assassination pulled the whole continent into disaster—in just a matter of weeks.

Postcards had already rehearsed the roles they would play in the conflict. During the "little" imperial wars of the 1890s and early 1900s, and especially during the Russo-Japanese War of 1904–5, illustrated postcards proved a major force in shaping public opinion and even reporting news. Domestic politics, too, played out on postcards. In France, the cards associated with the Dreyfus affair, which began in 1894, when the Jewish army officer Alfred Dreyfus was falsely accused and convicted of spying for Germany, were so numerous and influential that as early as 1903 they were the subject of a scholarly catalogue. So by the time the Great War came, artists, publishers, and governments had a full repertory of blustering nationalism, vicious insult, stirring patriotism, and mocking caricature on which to draw. Postcards were immediately put to work boosting morale and inciting anger on all sides.

The lighthearted tone of cards from the war's early months is almost shocking, as an expectation of quick victory on both sides led to designs that crackle

346 German storm surge, about 1914 UNGER (?)   347 With united forces! about 1914 VALERIE PETTER

with insouciance. Masses of German soldiers overrun France and cross the English Channel in a *Deutsche Sturmflut* (German storm surge), a sea of antlike men bearing a giant German military helmet [346]. (Presumably, it includes the soldier who, on another card, carries the Eiffel Tower home to mother as a souvenir [354].) Confidence ran nearly as high on the Allied side: a striking set of French cards from 1914 shows the opposing armies draped across Belgium and northern France as snakelike creatures with human heads. For months, the two writhe like wrestlers until the French front delivers a knockout blow to the Germans on November 10 [356–361]. The cartoon for that date probably refers to the Battle

of Langemarck, one episode in the month-long First Battle of Ypres—a killing field that left 135,000 men dead and wounded. That "decisive" battle was followed by another four years of war, and the doomed city of Ypres remained ensnared between the armies until the very last days of fighting in 1918.

The same themes played out on both sides of the war's divide. In France, a series of cards celebrates *nos héros* (our heroes) as noble young men—an aviator, a machine gunner, an artillery man—prepare to defend their country [348, 366–367]. In Germany, the cards Walter Georgi designed for the Bahlsen cookie company have much the same flavor: confident young soldiers remain vigilant and alert as they tend their

348 Our heroes. Foot soldier with machine gun, 1915

349 Leibniz cookies. On watch by the sea, 1914–15
WALTER GEORGI

weapons and keep watch (each with a package of Bahlsen's Leibniz cookies [349, 368–369]). Mockery and caricature were similar on both sides as well. For every arrogant and overreaching Kaiser Wilhelm on an Allied card, a German counterpart features a cowardly John Bull huddling on his navy's ships as he seeks to protect himself from German bombs with a very British "brolly" [370–371].

Similar events played differently on either side of the front, as one nation's glorious victory became the other's atrocity. The mockery that rings from a German card of a Frenchmen who desperately clings to the Eiffel Tower and brandishes a sign warning that bomb throwing is forbidden has a darker reflection

on Allied cards [355]. Early in the war, many cities in Belgium and northern France came under German attack, and the shelling of the great thirteenth-century French Gothic cathedral of Reims became a running theme. The monument was French, but the outrage was international: one Russian card shows the kaiser as a modern Nero who fiddles while Reims burns, the city's helpless citizens rushing to and fro as the catastrophe unfolds; an Italian card declares simply *"Deploriamo!"* (We deplore!) as the kaiser, morphed into a reptilian monster, crawls atop the rubble of the ruined cathedral [350–351].

Even as the war dragged on, some prewar patterns endured. Publishers still issued cards in series,

350 God's messenger, 1915 PIERRE CHATILLON

351 We deplore!!! about 1914 T.S.

and postcards still served traditional roles such as New Year's greetings. But many cards were now special editions, designed to be sent, postage-free, by soldiers from the front. The dramatic and stylish cards issued by the Bahlsen cookie factory are such *Feldpostkarten* (battlefield postcards), intended to advertise cookies even as they stir national pride. And just as before the war, images migrated freely from one format to another: poster designs appeared as postcards, and the snakelike creatures on the series of French cards from 1914 are borrowed from cartoons in the English magazine *The Bystander*. The postcard world even maintained some semblance of its cosmopolitan flavor at a time when international travel

was increasingly difficult: a number of British posters grace cards printed in Moscow on the occasion of an exhibition of Allied war posters [378–379].

As Europe staggered through the conflict, the years of destruction and economic disruption took their toll on the postcard trade, as on every other aspect of society. The postcard craze had begun to fade even before the war began, but by 1918 the fevered madness had passed almost completely. It is in the nature of fads to come and go on their own schedule, but by the end of the war the postcard mania may well have seemed to belong to a different age. Writing in 1919, the great British economist John Maynard Keynes looked back with wonderment at

378 (detail)

352 War savings stamps, 1917–18

353 Use the pieces, 1917–18

the innocence and blithe confidence that marked the decades before the catastrophe:

The inhabitant of London could order by telephone, sipping his morning tea in bed, the various products of the whole earth, in such quantity as he might see fit, and reasonably expect their early delivery upon his doorstep. . . . He could secure forthwith, if he wished it, cheap and comfortable means of transit to any country or climate without passport or other formality. . . . The projects and politics of militarism and imperialism, of racial and cultural rivalries, of monopolies, restrictions, and exclusion, which were to play the serpent to this paradise, were little more than the amusements of his daily newspaper, and appeared to exercise almost no influence at all on the ordinary course of social and economic life, the internationalization of which was nearly complete in practice.[1]

That was the world in which the postcard grew up. Although postcards endured and flourished in the decades after the Treaty of Versailles, the mood was different. The cards were never again the object of a lighthearted public crush the way they once had been. The world had changed.   B.W.

1. John Maynard Keynes, *The Economic Consequences of the Peace* (New York: Harcourt, Brace, and Howe, 1920), 12.

364 (detail)

354

355

354
Souvenir of Paris, about 1915
H. ZAHL

355
German doves over Paris, 1914

356–361
Battles of August–November, 1914

24 Aout

d'après "le Bystander".

356

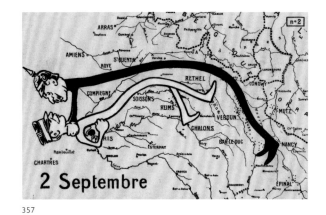

2 Septembre

357

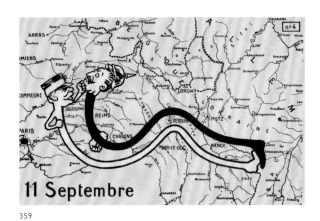

8 Septembre

358

11 Septembre

359

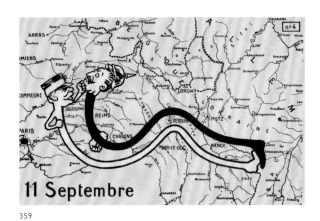

21 & 26 Septembre

360

10 Novembre

361

362

362

The dream. The reality,
about 1918

J. DELENA

363

Mine, all mine, and God's,
about 1918

363

Peccato che non riesco a soffocarla

364

L'INGORDO
TROP DUR

365

364
Too bad I cannot suffocate it, about 1918
R. FERROI(?)

365
The glutton. Too hard, about 1914
GOLIA (EUGENIO COLMO)

366

Our heroes, 1915

366
Aviator

367
Artilleryman

367

Leibniz cookies, 1914–15
WALTER GEORGI

368
Airmen

369
Torpedo boat at full speed

368

369

Die englische Krankheit!

370

Hoch über Englands Länder hin
Streifen die deutschen Zeppelin,
John Bull sitzt auf den Schifflein drauf
Und spannt zum Schutz den Schirm sich auf.

371

370
The English disease!
about 1914
LEONARD

371
John Bull on his little ships,
about 1914
W.S. OR T.S.

Какъ обезумѣвшій сатиръ,
Вильгельмъ всѣхъ морочитъ,—
Въ пылу безумья цѣлый міръ
Залить онъ кровью хочетъ.

372

372

Wilhelm . . . wants to flood the entire
world with blood, 1914–17

T.

373

The Nero of our times, 1914–17

T.

НЕРОНЪ НАШИХЪ ДНЕЙ.

373

374–375

German armaments,
1915 and 1916

CARL OTTO CZESCHKA

374

375

376

Masters of the air,
about 1914

HEINZ KEUNE

377

Our navy,
about 1914

HEINZ KEUNE

376

377

378

British recruiting posters, 1915 and 1916

378
"Daddy, what did *you* do in the Great War?"
1916
SAVILE LUMLEY

379
Women of Britain say—"Go!"
1916
E. V. KEALEY

380
"You are the man I want,"
about 1915

379

380

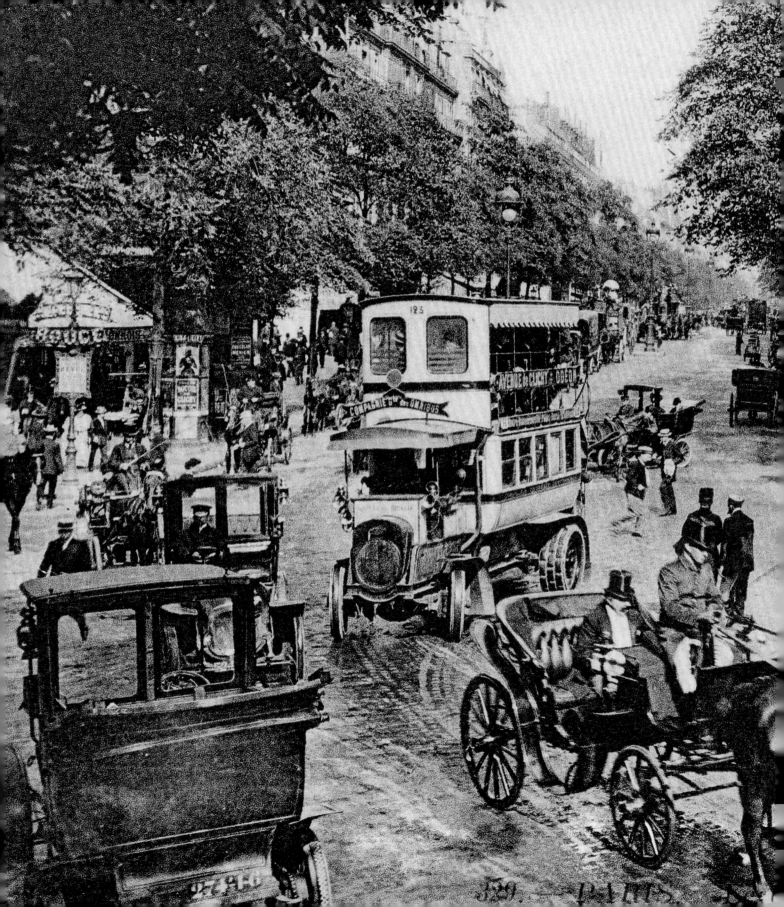

LIST OF ILLUSTRATIONS

ANNA JOZEFACKA, LYNDA KLICH, AND BENJAMIN WEISS

with contributions from Jocelyn Elliott, Luise Mahler, Anne Nishimura Morse, Samuel C. Morse, and Anya Pantuyeva

As we have researched the cards in this book, we have found that determining when, why, and even by whom some were made can be a matter of luck. For others, we have far more information than could ever fit here. More details about many of these cards are available in the MFA's collections database, at *www.mfa.org/collections*. The Lauder Archive contains about a hundred thousand cards, and the process of cataloguing is ongoing. Please do not hesitate to contact the authors (*LauderArchive@mfa.org*) if you have information to contribute to this effort.

The size of postcards was standardized by international regulations almost from the very beginning, so unless otherwise noted all of the cards reproduced in this book are 9 x 14 cm (3½ x 5½ in.).

Unless stated otherwise, all cards are from the Leonard A. Lauder Postcard Archive, a promised gift to the Museum of Fine Arts, Boston.

I
Der Bombenwerfer Čabrinovič
(The bomb-thrower Čabrinovič), 1914
Published in Vienna by Verlag Philipp Rubel
Real photograph on card stock (divided back)

2
From your soldier boy, about 1915
Embroidery on card stock

3
La bandiera futurista (The Futurist flag);
Marciare, non marcire (March, don't rot), 1915
Hand decoration by Giacomo Balla (Italian, 1871–1958)
Opaque watercolor and ink applied to color lithograph on card stock
Collection of Leonard A. Lauder
Copyright © 2012 Artist Rights Society (ARS), New York/SIAE, Rome

4
Eiffel Tower, 1889
Léon-Charles Libonis (French, 1846–1901)
Published in Paris
Lithograph (undivided back)

5
Paris—Tour Eiffel (Paris—Eiffel Tower), before 1904
Published in Paris by C.L.C. (Charles l'Hôpital et Cie.), no. 114
Photolithograph (undivided back)

6
Paris.—La Tour Eiffel, Galerie extérieure du premier Étage (Paris.—The Eiffel Tower, exterior gallery of the first level), after 1903
Published in Paris by N.D. (Neurdein Frères), no. 1019
Photolithograph (divided back)

7
Paris.—La Tour Eiffel, Platforme du deuxième Étage (Paris.—The Eiffel Tower, platform of the second level), after 1903
Published in Paris by N.D. (Neurdein Frères), no. 1021
Photolithograph (divided back)

8
Paris. La Tour Eiffel, Galerie extérieure du deuxième étage (Paris. The Eiffel Tower, exterior gallery of the second level), after 1903
Published in Paris by N.D. (Neurdein Frères), no. 1020
Photolithograph (divided back)

9
Grand Café, after 1903
Published in France by A. Detrèfle (?)
Real photograph on card stock (divided back)

10
Boucherie L. Dupont. 5 rue Guersant, Paris (L. Dupont's Butcher Shop), after 1903
Published in France
Real photograph on card stock (divided back)

II
Paris.—Le Boulevard Montmartre, carrefou[r] Drouot (Paris.—Boulevard Montmartre, intersection Drouot), after 1903
Published in Paris by N.D. (Neurdein Frères), no. 329
Photolithograph (divided back)

12
Paris—Rue Mouffetard, after 1903
Published in Paris by L.L. (Louis Lévy et fils),
no. 949
Photolithograph (divided back)

13
Exposition Universelle de 1900.—Théâtre
des Bonshommes Guillaume. (La Frise)
(Universal Exposition of 1900.—Theater of
the Guillaume boys. [The frieze]), 1900
Albert-André Guillaume (French, 1873–1942)
Published in Paris by Courmont Frères
Color lithograph (undivided back)

One of the most popular side attractions at
the 1900 Universal Exposition was the
Guillaume brothers' theater, where puppets
acted out scenes from Parisian life. This card
shows part of the building's painted frieze.

14
La Burgeatine, la plus exquise des liqueurs
de table (La Burgeatine, the most exquisite
digestif), about 1900
Nover
Published in Paris by L. Revon & Cie.
Color lithograph (undivided back)

"Nover" is a palindrome of Revon, publisher
of this card; the artist was likely Monsieur
Revon himself or an employee of the firm.

15–16
Parisian women, about 1900
Carlos Bady
Published in Paris by G.H., series no. 39
Color lithographs (divided back)

17
Der alte St. Gotthard (Old Saint Gotthard),
1897
Emil Hansen (Emil Nolde) (German,
1867–1956)
Published in Zurich by F. Killinger
Color lithograph (undivided back)

Nolde was not the first to give human names
to the Alps, but he does seem to have been
the first to design postcards of the personified
mountains. The Saint Gotthard massif is
named for the eleventh-century bishop of

Hildesheim—hence the halo. It was one of the
earliest Swiss peaks to be pierced by a railroad
tunnel, shown here emerging from between
the saint's hiking boots.

18
La favorite, no. 2, 1900
Raphael Kirchner (Austrian, 1876–1917)
Published in Vienna by Emile Storch
Color lithograph and metallic pigment on
card stock

19
See figs. 44–46

20
Frog puzzle, about 1900
Published in New York by Walter Wirths
Art Co.
Color lithographs (undivided back)

Though these cards are meant to be a puzzle,
the designer provided a poem as a clue; it
begins on the middle, and most mysterious
card, which was to be mailed first. Although
the cards were probably designed and
produced in Germany, the backs of this set
are printed for use in the United States mails.

He who admires this work of art
Regrets to find it just a part—

At once it's clear what it must be:
An insect-snapping frog, you see.

So now you know how it will end,
Another dime has been well spent.

21
Cat puzzle, about 1900
Printed in Germany
Color lithographs (undivided back)

22
Stork puzzle, about 1900
Printed in Germany
Color lithographs (undivided back)

23
La Cartolinomania (Postcard mania),
about 1905
Van Dock (Vincenzo Nasi)

Published by G.F. & C., no. 16
Color lithograph (undivided back)

Nasi uses a monocle and upturned moustache
to lampoon a favorite target of postcard
writers: obsessive German collectors.

24
Membership card, Carto-Philatélique Club,
about 1904
Orens Denizard (French, 1879–1965)
Published in Paris by *Le carto-philatélique journal*
Lithograph (undivided back)

25
Marseille—Camelots vendant les cartes
postales (Marseille—peddlers selling
postcards), about 1910
Published in Marseille by E. Lacour, no. 2496
Hand-colored photolithograph (divided back)

26
Amateurs et collectionneurs (Enthusiasts and
collectors), about 1900
Published in Nancy, France, by A. Bergeret
et Cie.
Photolithograph (undivided back)

Founded in 1886, Albert Bergeret's photo
studio issued hundreds of millions of postcards
after 1898. Among its specialties were cards
that poked fun at postcard enthusiasts; the
staged photograph here captures a pair of
tourists as they peruse the offerings on a postcard rack.

27
La carte postale entretient l'amitié (The
postcard maintains friendship), about 1904
Published in Nancy, France, by A. Bergeret
et Cie.
Photolithograph (undivided back)

28
Les voyageurs en cartes postales (Postcard
tourists), about 1900
Published in Brussels by Marco Marcovici,
no. 7415
Color lithograph (undivided back)

Victims of the postcard craze line up at the
postcard shop, albums in hand, while others

depart carrying lengthy scrolls that recount their orders. This card is from Belgium, so the crowd is bilingual: the fellow in the straw hat peruses a sheet headed "Bestell"; in front of him, the one in the top hat holds his "Commande."

29
Boulogne-sur-Mer. Publicité locale hors concours (Local advertising without competition), about 1905
Published in Boulogne-sur-Mer, France, by E.S., no. 193
Photolithograph (divided back)

30
La carte postale (The postcard), about 1900
Published in Nancy, France, by A. Bergeret et Cie.
Photolithograph (undivided back)

Armand Gaboriaud was one of the "house poets" for the publisher Bergeret. A rough translation:

All about our orb so round,
The picture postcard doth abound;
All the publishers so inventive
Strive as well to be instructive.
Which is the best in France?
This mystery we shall see;
I say, with no hesitance,
It is Bergeret, of Nancy.

31
La collectionneuse (The collector), about 1909
Georges Morinet (French, active 1900–at least 1915)
Published in Nancy, France, by A. Bergeret et Cie.
Photolithograph (divided back)

A seductive woman entices the collector: "Send me postcards, and you will always bring me pleasure."

32
Demandez les cartes postales illustrées editées par la Croix-Rouge (Ask for the illustrated postcards published by the Red Cross), 1904
Léon Bakst (Russian, 1866–1924)

Published in Saint Petersburg by the Community of Saint Eugenia for the Saint Petersburg Committee of the Red Cross; printed in Saint Petersburg by Isaac Kadushkin
Poster; color lithograph
46.3 x 62.2 cm (18¼ x 24½ in.)
Collection of Leonard A. Lauder
Courtesy of Posters Please, Inc., New York

In 1904 the Community of Saint Eugenia, a Saint Petersburg–based charitable organization, commissioned Bakst to create a poster to promote postcards designed by Russian artists that would be sold to benefit the Red Cross.

33
Ansichts Karten-Ausstellung. Weihnachts und Neujahrs Karten (Exhibition of view cards. Christmas and New Year's cards), after 1898
T. H. or H. T. Bauer
Published in Vienna by B.K.W. (Brüder Kohn Wien); printed in Vienna by the Gesellschaft für Graphische Industrie
Poster; color lithograph
99.1 x 61.9 cm (39 x 24⅜ in.)
Collection of Leonard A. Lauder
Courtesy of Posters Please, Inc., New York

Cards flutter down from a balloon that bears the slogan "Bediene dich selbst" (Help yourself!), as a young man in postal uniform directs viewers to the three stores run by Brüder Kohn, one of Vienna's leading postcard publishers. Salomon, Adolf, and Alfred Kohn started the company in 1898 and remained in business until 1938, when the firm was Aryanized after the Anschluss. Brüder Kohn promoted the work of some of the best-known artists associated with postcards, including Raphael Kirchner and Mela Koehler. The placard offers customers a "höchst interessant" (most interesting) free tour of the stores.

34
Salon des Arts Lithographiques et de la Carte Postale Illustrée (Salon of art lithographs and illustrated postcards), about 1900
William-Adolphe Lambrecht (French, 1876–1940)
Published in Toulouse, France, by B. Sirven
Poster; color lithograph
139.7 x 99.5 cm (55 x 39⅛ in.)

Collection of Leonard A. Lauder
Courtesy of Posters Please, Inc., New York

35–37
From a series for the Universal Exposition, 1900
Published in France
Color lithographs (undivided back)

38
Le tour du monde (Around the World); Paris. Exposition de 1900
Published in Paris by SMA, no. 21
Color lithographs (undivided back)

39
Palais de l'électricité (Champ de Mars). Exposition Universelle 1900 (Palace of Electricity [Champ de Mars]), 1900
Patented by s.g.d.g.; published in Paris by Kann Frères & Zabern
Die-cut color lithograph (undivided back)

40–41
Postcard-tickets to the 1900 Universal Exposition in Paris, 1899
Published in Paris
Color lithographs (undivided back)

42
Le passe-partout de l'Exposition 1900. Paris (All-access pass to the Exposition 1900. Paris), 1899
G. Guidi
Published in Paris by Courmont Frères
Book of 36 postcard-tickets
Color lithographs (undivided back)

43
Globe céleste (Celestial Globe). Chocolat Suchard. Exposition Universelle de Paris 1900 (Suchard Chocolate. Universal Exposition Paris), 1900
Published in Paris by Chocolat Suchard, no. 6
Color lithograph (undivided back)

44–46
College girls and boys, 1907
F. Earl Christy (American, 1883–1961)
Published in New York by Julius Bien & Company, series no. 95
Color lithographs (divided back)

47
Woman on a paper moon, about 1910
S. M. John
Printed in Kenton, Ohio
Real photograph on card stock (divided back)

48
Man on a paper moon, about 1910
Printed in the United States
Real photograph on card stock (divided back)

During the early twentieth century, photography studios often offered fantastical settings for their portraits. Paper moons were among the most requested props.

49
Pavillon für Karten von Professor Olbrich. Ausstellung Künstler-Kolonie Darmstadt (Professor Olbrich's postcard pavilion. Darmstadt Artists' Colony Exhibition), 1901
Hans Christiansen (German, 1866–1945)
Published in Frankfurt am Main by Kunst-Anstalt Kornsand & Co.
Color lithograph

50
Cartes postales artistiques, éditions Dietrich & Cie. Bruxelles (Artistic postcards published by Dietrich & Company, Brussels), 1898
Henri Meunier (Belgian, 1873–1922)
Published in Brussels by Dietrich & Cie.; printed in Brussels by Affiches d'art O. Rycker
74.2 x 94.5 cm (29¼ x 37¼ in.)
Poster; color lithograph
Collection of Leonard A. Lauder
Photograph: James McCobb

Meunier was among a group of artists from whom the Belgian fine art publisher Dietrich and Company commissioned postcard series beginning in 1898. The series were exhibited widely and highly sought after by collectors. This poster advertises the new products and the firm's Brussels shop.

51–53
See figs. 77–79

54–55
Ver Sacrum. Erste grosse Kunstausstellung der Vereinigung bildender Künstler Oesterreichs.

Secession (Sacred Spring. First great art exhibition of the Artists' Association of Austria. Secession), 1898
Koloman Moser (Austrian, 1868–1918) and Josef Hoffmann (Austrian, 1870–1956)
Published in Vienna by Verlag von Gerlach & Schenk, card nos. 3 and 4
Color lithographs with gold ink (undivided back)

The Secessionists adopted the Latin phrase *ver sacrum* (sacred spring) to express their goal of artistic rejuvenation. As in these cards, they encouraged artistic collaboration as a means to that end. Despite their reputation as nonconformists, the Secession artists complied with postal regulations for the size and format of the postcards.

56–57
Mädchenköpfe zwischen Rosen (Girls' heads among roses), issued for the Ausstellung Künstler-Kolonie Darmstadt (Darmstadt Artists' Colony Exhibition), 1901
Hans Christiansen (German, 1866–1945)
Published in Frankfurt am Main by Kunst-Anstalt Kornsand & Co.
Color lithographs (undivided back)

Christiansen was one of seven artists enlisted by the Grand Duke of Hesse to form an artists' colony at Darmstadt in 1899. These cards, which feature the artist's signature rose motif, were sold in a kiosk set up on the colony's grounds (see fig. 49). Christiansen understood how effective postcards could be in promoting the Duke's undertaking; in 1894 he had designed a series of eighteen humorous postcards, all featuring the common postcard phrase "Gruss aus Hamburg" (Greetings from Hamburg). By captioning the 1901 cards simply "Darmstadt," Christiansen blurred the line between the ordinary greeting postcard and the artist postcard.

58–61
La Fotografia (Photography), about 1900
Luigi Bompard (Italian, 1879–1953)
Published in Bologna by Edit. Giovanni Mengoli
Color lithographs (undivided back)

Son of a French merchant and an Italian photographer, Bompard was a self-taught graphic designer who worked with publishers in both Paris and Bologna.

62–63
Fashionable people, about 1906
Ilona (Hélène) Máté (Hungarian, 1887–1908)
Published in London by M. Ettlinger & Company (as series no. 4548) and printed in Belgium; also published in France by C. T. & Cie. (as series no. 113)
Color lithographs (undivided back)

Publishers in various countries issued Máté's cards of fashion-conscious, wealthy urbanites. Striking in their economy of form and color, the compositions' up-to-date cropping techniques suggest quick snapshots of the modern world.

64–66
Months of the year (also published as Women and as Sports), about 1900
Franz Laskoff (Franciszek Laskowski) (Polish, worked in Italy, 1869–1918)
Published in Milan by Officine Grafiche Ricordi & Company
Color lithographs (undivided back)

A graduate of the Kunstgewerbeschule (Arts and Crafts School) in Strasbourg, Laskoff worked for publishers in France, Great Britain, and Italy. Each card in this series pairs the tightly framed profile of a fashionably dressed woman with a distant view of an everyday activity.

67–68
III. Zürcher Raumkunst Ausstellung (Third Zurich Interior Design Show), 1911–12
Jószef Divéky (Hungarian, 1887–1951)
Printed in Zurich by Graphische Anstalt J. E Wolfensberger
Color lithographs (undivided back)

A prolific designer who distinguished himself as a member of the Wiener Werkstätte (Viennese Workshops), Divéky created these cards for an exhibition at Zurich's Kunstgewerbemuseum (Arts and Crafts Museum, now the Museum für Gestaltung). The post-cards capture the museum's mission by depicting furniture, applied arts objects, and flower arrangements, while themselves being examples of design.

69–70
Femmes mondaines (Women of the world), about 1900
Árpád Basch (Hungarian, 1873–1944)
Unknown publisher, series no. 653
Color lithographs with gold ink and embossing (undivided back)

Basch's schooling took him from his native Hungary to France, Germany, Italy, and England. He eventually settled back in Budapest, becoming influential in local artistic circles.

71–72
Scenes from Russian epic poems, 1901
Ivan (Yakovlevich) Bilibin (Russian, 1876–1942)
Published in Saint Petersburg by the Community of Saint Eugenia, for the Saint Petersburg Committee of the Red Cross; printed by A. Ilyin
Color lithographs (divided back)

These images derive from Bilibin's illustrations for Russian folk epics. The hero of the tale of Oleg recruited peasant warriors to fight alongside aristocrats in defending Russia against Baltic invaders. Sadko, a mythical musician turned merchant, lived in the city of Novgorod, where the prince shared rule with a democratic council. Both stories glorify the role of Russian commoners in the formation of the nation, giving the cards a mild antimonarchist flavor.

71. Vol'ga (Oleg). The young warriors are riding in a vast field. They are riding from dawn till dusk.

72. Sadko. Long live the great and free city of Novgorod!

73–74
Costumes for *Boris Godunov*, 1908
Ivan (Yakovlevich) Bilibin (Russian, 1876–1942)
Published in Saint Petersburg by the Community of the Sisters of Mercy of Saint

Eugenia, for the Saint Petersburg Committee of the Red Cross; printed in Saint Petersburg by N. Kadushkin

Bibilin designed these costumes for a production of Modest Mussorgsky's opera that was produced by Serge Diaghilev at the Théâtre national de l'Opéra in Paris. The cards, which recall medieval manuscript illustrations, are identified by captions in the cartouches that hover next to the figures.

75–76
Les signes du zodiaque (Signs of the zodiac), 1898
Henri Meunier (Belgian, 1873–1922)
Published in Brussels by Dietrich & Cie.
Color lithographs (undivided back)

Dietrich commissioned these designs from Meunier for their line of Cartes postales artistiques (Artistic postcards). The company's high-quality printing, such as the eye-catching silver ink on this set, reinforced the cutting-edge graphics. Meunier rendered the astrological signs in three distinct pictorial languages: as arrangements of stars, as personifications, and, below the "window," by their symbols.

77–79
Les éléments (The elements), 1898
Gisbert Combaz (Belgian, 1869–1941)
Published in Brussels by Dietrich & Cie.
Color lithographs (undivided back)

For this series, Combaz adapted designs he had made for ceramic tiles as well as book and magazine illustrations. The stylized forms and unconventional relationships between the figures and the background recall Japanese woodblock prints, a frequent source of inspiration for avant-garde artists in the second half of the nineteenth century.

80
"Moderne," from a series of cards showing dance through the ages, 1900
Ernest Louis Lessieux (French, 1848–1925)
Color lithograph (undivided back)

81–82
Berlin sights, 1912
Walter Buhe (German, 1882–1958)
Published in Berlin for the Deutsche Lehrerversammlung (German Teachers' Assembly)
Color lithographs (divided back)

These views of famous Berlin sights were meant as souvenirs for the attendees of a teachers' conference. Buhe seems to have based his designs directly on photographic postcards of the same scenes.

83
Luna Park. Le Scenic Raillway, passage d'une courbe au sommet du Pikes Peakes (Luna Park. The scenic railway traversing a curve at the top of Pike's Peak), after 1909
Published in Paris by Neurdein et Cie., no. 33
Real photograph on card stock (divided back)

84
Luna Park.—Scenic railway. Massif Nord. Rampe courbe d'accès au point culminant (Luna Park.—Scenic Railway. North Massif. Curved ramp reaching the highest point), after 1909
Printed in Paris by Neurdein et Cie.
Real photograph on card stock (divided back)

85–86
Dresden street scenes, about 1900
Published in Dresden by Erika, series no. 3378
Color lithographs (divided back)

87–88
Wiener Typen (Viennese types), 1897–99
Raphael Kirchner (Austrian, 1876–1917)
Probably published in Vienna
Color lithographs (undivided back)

89–90
Bal du Moulin Rouge. Tous les soirs à 9 hres (Moulin Rouge. Every night at 9 o'clock), about 1905
Charles Naillod (French, 1876–1956)
Published in France
Color lithographs (divided back)

91–94
Women of the Paris stage, 1901
Published in Paris by S.I.P (Société industrielle
de la photographie)
Photolithographs (undivided back)

91. Armande Cassive with a poster for the
Théâtre des Nouveautés's production of Paul
Bilhaud and Maurice Hennequin's *Nelly Rozier*
(no. 6)

92. Marthe Brandès with a poster for the
Comédie-Française's production of Paul
Hervieu's *L'énigme* (no. 5)

93. Jeanne Bloch (?) with a poster for *À nous la
veine*, for the *café-concert* La Cigale (no. 20)

94. Germaine Gallois with a poster for the
café-concert La Scala (no. 1)

This series presents a snapshot of the Paris
theatrical world in December 1901. The cards
feature a mix of serious actresses, dancers,
and singers, and the theaters range right up
and down the scale of prestige and respectability. If fig. 93 does indeed show the comic
singer Jeanne Bloch in *À nous la veine*, the
image immortalizes a show that Pablo Picasso
saw during his early years in Paris.

95–96
Saint-Sauveur, Bruxelles, about 1910
S. Bailie
Published and printed in Brussels by O. de
Rycker & Mendel
Color lithograph (divided back)

The back of the card with the skating scene
includes a reproduction of a short newspaper
article announcing that the rink at the Bains
has reopened, with a tearoom that has
become "more and more the rendezvous for
the *high-life Bruxellois*."

97–98
Poster Views of New York, 1924
Published in New York by A. Broun; printed in
Germany
Color lithographs (divided back)

99
Das Liebes-Sanatorium. Burlesk-Operette von
Rudolf Báron (The Love Hospital. Burlesque
operetta by Rudolf Báron), 1912
Georg Caré
Published in Berlin by Reklameverlag
Ernst Marx
Color lithograph (divided back)

100
Rollschuhbahn (Roller skating rink),
about 1910
Friedrich ("Fritz") Carl Georg Rumpf
(German, 1888–1949)
Published in Berlin by Curt Behrends
Color lithograph (divided back)

101
Grand Café Schöneberg, about 1914
Michel Noa
Printed in Berlin by Atelier Jaretzky
Color lithograph (divided back)

The Grand Café was one of the larger cafés
along the main street of the Berlin neighbor-
hood of Schöneberg.

102
Trocadero, about 1910
Friedrich ("Fritz") Carl Georg Rumpf
(German, 1888–1949)
Published in Berlin by Curt Behrends
Color lithograph (divided back)

With a name borrowed from Paris and a card
designed and printed in Berlin, the Trocadero
asserts its place as Hamburg's "most genteel
establishment." The club was located on a
main street that ran to Hamburg's scenic
inner harbor.

103–104
Cards reproducing posters for the Sarrasani
Circus, about 1928
Published in Heidenau, Germany, by Mittel-
deutsche Verlagsanstalt GmbH; printed in
Munich by Vereinigte Druckereien
Color lithographs (divided back)

105–107
Zoologischer Garten, Basel (Basel zoo),
about 1922
Hedwig Keerl Thoma (Swiss, 1886–1946)
Probably published in Basel
Color lithographs (divided back)

108–109
"The slide" and "Riding the elephant" at Luna
Park, Coney Island, N.Y., about 1910
Published in New York by Joseph Koehler;
printed in Berlin
Die-cut color lithographs (divided back)

Pleasure grounds like Luna Park, which
presented a dazzling display of electric lights,
were natural subjects for hold-to-light cards.
Like nearly all such cards, these were printed
in Germany.

110–111
Luna Park, 1910
Hans Kalmsteiner (Austrian, 1882–about
1914)
Published and printed in Vienna for the
I. Internationale Jagd-Ausstellung (First
international hunting exhibition) by Patzelt
& Cie.
Color lithographs (divided back)

112
Fleurs d'amour (Flowers of love), about 1900
Raphael Kirchner (Austrian, 1876–1917)
Color lithograph (undivided back)

113
La question est posée: portera-t-on la
jupe-pantalon en 1911? (The question is
posed: Will they wear culottes in 1911?)
Published in Paris by N.D. (Neurdein Frères)
Collotype (divided back)

114–116
"Motoring," "In the library," and "Late autumn"
"In the library," and "Late autumn" signed
by M. C.
"Motoring" published in London by Raphael
Tuck & Sons and printed in Germany; "In the
library" and "Late autumn" published in Paris
by Raphael Tuck et fils., set no. 1369
Color lithographs (divided back)

The artist who produced these cards combined the latest design strategies, such as cropping and heavy black outlining, with the equally up-to-date subject of the sophisticated and fashionable new woman. The series was issued in Great Britain with the title "Modern Art," and in France as "Modern Style." Another title for the series was "Girl of the Period."

117
Les premières femmes colleuses d'affiches
(The first women poster hangers), about 1908
Collotype (divided back)

In Paris, female poster hangers attracted great attention, drawing crowds—mainly of men—as they worked along the city's boulevards. The label of Publicité Gabert on their hats identifies the advertising agency that probably employed the women and staged the scenes for the postcards.

118
La première femme colleuse d'affiches
(The first woman poster hanger), about 1908
J. H.
No. 926
Collotype (divided back)

119–120
From the series Paris moderne (Modern Paris), about 1908
Published and printed in Paris by N.D. (Neurdein et Cie.)
Photolithographs (divided back)

Female taxi drivers first took to Parisian streets in February 1907. Many were aristocratic women who had fallen on hard times, and they become favorite subjects of the press. Madame Decourcelle, the driver shown in fig. 120, was among the first to switch to a motorized taxi.

119. Woman taxi driver. Ticketed for speeding in the Bois de Boulogne. Speeding because of a customer in a hurry, our poor woman driver could not escape the attention of a guard; a ticket will remind her that in the Bois, speed is to be moderated.

120. Woman taxi driver, starting the car. Watching her take hold of the crank, you fear for her back. Do not worry, she has nerves of steel; she will achieve compression and turn over the motor on the first try.

121–124
Women wearing muzzles, before 1914
Printed in Germany by H.W.B. or H.B.W., series no. 8851
Color lithographs with slight embossing (divided back)

125–126
À travers Paris (Around Paris), about 1900–1910
François Xavier Sager (French, about 1881–1969)
Published in Paris by B.M., series no. 503
Color lithographs (divided back)

Based in Paris, Sager designed an estimated three thousand postcards, printed in numbers that total more than three million. These cards are typical of Sager's work, combining the flowing lines of fashion illustration with lively scenes that highlight risqué aspects of Parisian life. The series also appeared under the title Paris s'amuse (Paris entertains itself).

127–128
Valentine postcards from the series Poster Girls, after 1902
B
Published in London and printed in Berlin by Raphael Tuck & Sons, set no. 231
Color lithographs (divided back)

129–131
Curiosités-Parisiennes (Parisian sights), 1905
C. Fox
Colored lithographs, hand colored (divided back)

Fox is most likely a pseudonym for the designer of a group of satirical and erotic postcard series, any one of which would have put him and his publisher in trouble with the law. The more than thirty cards in this set marry Parisian monuments to lewd drawings of the city's celebrated can-can dancers and prostitutes. The poem on the card depicting

the Great Wheel invites the recipient to go "round and round," en route to many "inside" attractions.

132
Two men and a woman, about 1900
No. 81 U
Color lithograph (undivided back)

133
A man and a woman, about 1900
Published by C.C. & M.B., no. 17
Color lithograph (undivided back)

134
Die Jungfrau, about 1905
Printed and published in Zurich by W. Pleyer's Photo & Karten-Centrale, no. 195-89
Color lithograph (divided back)

The peak of the Jungfrau rises behind a reclining woman whose slopes are traversed by four miniscule men. Around the time this postcard was published, a railway eased the climb by delivering tourists to a spot just below the summit.

135–136
Photomontages of nude women on neckties, 1911
Martin Gerlach (1846–1918) and Martin Gerlach, Jr. (1879–1944)
Published and printed in Vienna by Gerlach and Gerlach & Co., series 1512, nos. 3 and 6
Real photographs on card stock (divided back)

Produced by a father-and-son team, these cards typify the manipulated imagery that attracted avant-garde artists like the Dadaists and Surrealists to postcard collecting in the 1920s.

137–139
Continental Pneumatic, about 1900
Published and printed in Germany by Continental-Caoutchouc und Gutta-Percha Compagnie
Color lithographs (undivided back)

The Continental Rubber Company contributed to both the bicycle and the postcard crazes, issuing numerous series of advertising cards that also poked fun at the unsettling modern world. These cards feature women wearing bloomers so they can straddle the bar of a bicycle. Not only are the women wearing pants in public, they also have the nerve to drink, experiment with cameras, and tour the countryside unaccompanied by a man.

140
Beer mug, undated
Published in Berlin by Fabrik Marke
Color lithograph (divided back)

"Mechanical" postcards, with moving parts such as pull tabs, pop-ups, or turning wheels, were a favored novelty among collectors. Pull the tab at the bottom of this beer stein and out pops a scantily dressed maiden, holding a beer of her own. The jolly message translates, roughly: "I know what would refresh you, so I send you this today. Now, dear friend, with all my heart I wish you—Cheers!"

141–142
Women modeling hats, about 1910
Melanie (Mela) Koehler (Austrian, 1885–1960)
Printed in Vienna by B.K.W., series no. 481
Color lithographs (divided back)

143–144
Women with small dogs, about 1910
Melanie (Mela) Koehler (Austrian, 1885–1960)
Printed in Vienna by B.K.W., series no. 621, nos. 3 and 6
Color lithographs (divided back)

Koehler's postcards were just one aspect of a design career that also embraced fashion illustration, ceramics, and textiles; many of those designs also appear on her postcards. Koehler almost always worked in series. These cards are from one of many sets published by Brüder Kohn that feature stylish accessories such as hats and even lapdogs.

145–148
Blanche-noir (White-black), 1920s
Signed with a monogram that includes AGS, W, and KKM
Published in Salzburg, Austria, by F. Morawetz; printed in Innsbruck, Austria, by Wagner
Lithographs (divided back)

The bold designs in these fashion postcards display an affinity with the work of the Vienna Secession. The coat in fig. 148, for example, shows the *Jagdfalke* (gyrfalcon) pattern designed by Josef Hoffmann for the Wiener Werkstätte in 1910–11.

149–150
Champ de courses d'Auteuil (Auteuil racecourse), about 1912
Published in Paris by Neurdein et Cie., nos. 1 and 7
Real photograph on card stock (divided back)

The Auteuil hippodrome in the Bois de Boulogne specialized in steeplechase races. Since opening in 1873, it had drawn large crowds to its four major races each year, and the women who attended were considered to be fashion trendsetters. These cards capture summer ensembles worn "in the paddock" and "in front of the stands."

151–154
Fashion in 1909, from the series Le sourire (The smile), 1909
André-Félix Roberty (French, 1877–1963)
Hand-colored lithographs (divided back)

155–156
See figs. 160–161

157
Czar Nicholas II and family in a rowboat, before 1917
Real photograph on card stock (divided back)

158–159
Jan Olieslagers and Glenn Hammond Curtiss, from the series Modern-oiseaux (Modern birds), about 1910
César Giris (Cesare Giri) (Italian, worked in France, 1877–1941)
Published or printed by L.B.
Color lithographs (divided back)

160–161
Caricatures of royalty, 1903
Geo (Henri Jules Jean Geoffroy) (French, 1853–1924)

Fabric, ink, paper, and sequins on card stock (undivided back)

155. Wilhelm II, emperor of Germany

156. The Shah of Persia

160. Leopold II, king of Belgium

161. Edward VII, king of the United Kingdom

Despite their charm, the gallery of what the French postcard journal *Cartophile* called "stuffed sovereigns" that Geoffroy and other artists such as Henri Pierre created in the years just after 1900 was not universally popular. Some collectors reportedly considered the collages "not-so-serious trinkets" in comparison with more traditional drawn or engraved caricatures.

162
Theodore Roosevelt, about 1905
P.P.
Fabric, ink, and paper on card stock (undivided back)

163
Czar Nicholas II, about 1905
Henri Pierre
Published in Paris
Fabric, ink, paper, sequins, and metallic cord on card stock (undivided back)

164
Kniaz-Potemkine. La torche brûle . . . c'est fini (*Prince Potemkin. The torch burns . . . it's over*), 1905
Orens Denizard (French, 1879–1965)
No. 56 from the series Actualité satirique (Satirical news)
Hand-colored lithograph (divided back)

The seizure of the Black Sea battleship *Prince Potemkin* by its crew was one of the most important events in the chain of strikes and rebellions during the First Russian Revolution of 1905. The mutiny was unsuccessful, but the event showed that the very foundation of the czar's power was shattering.

165
La bougie Russe (The Russian candle), 1905
Orens Denizard (French, 1879–1965)

Published in France by F & J, no. 3 from the series L'actualiste (The current)
Hand-colored lithograph (divided back)

The Russian candle whose flame will soon gutter and go out is, of course, Czar Nicholas II—neatly labeled, in case one might miss the point.

166
Rasputin, about 1912
Color lithograph (divided back)

167
Rasputin, about 1917
W.
No. 62
Lithograph (unprinted back)

During the mid-1910s Russia witnessed a concerted political campaign against Grigory Rasputin, a peasant and religious pilgrim widely believed to hold extraordinary power over Czar Nicholas II and his wife, Alexandra Fyodorovna. Russians from all sectors of society opposed him. His wild appearance in these cards perhaps reflects the belief among the peasant and working classes that he held diabolical powers; by contrast, conservative pro-monarchy circles mainly objected to the influence Rasputin wielded over the royals. He was assassinated in December 1916. The card shown in fig.166 suggests that Rasputin actually has usurped the czar's crown, while fig. 167 shows Rasputin playing with a common wooden toy. In place of the traditional battling bear and peasant figurines, the czar and a priest (representing the Russian Orthodox Church) fight over old heroic Russia, personified by the oversized head of a Russian warrior in a medieval helmet.

168
Roosevelt.—Assez! C'est déjà le temps de partager . . . (Roosevelt.—Enough! It's time to share), about 1905
Tomás Júlio Leal da Câmara (Portuguese, 1877–1948)
Published in Paris by B.C.I., no. 48 in the series Le carillon
Hand-colored lithograph (divided back)

169
Mr. Roosevelt sépare les combatants (Mr. Roosevelt separates the combatants), 1905
Mille
Published in France, by F & J, no. 22 in the series L'arc en ciel (The rainbow)
Hand-colored lithograph (divided back)

170
Pax. L'attitude de Mr. Roosevelt (Peace. The position of Mr. Roosevelt), 1905
F. Marmonier
Published in Paris by B.C.I., no. 60 in the series Le carillon
Hand-colored lithograph (divided back)

The United States took an unprecedented place on the world stage when President Theodore Roosevelt brokered an end to the Russo-Japanese War in September 1905. Here, Roosevelt—as saint or bully—serves as buffer between the combatants. Roosevelt's depiction reflects a growing uneasiness about increasing U.S. power and wealth. Leal da Câmara's version of the scene (fig. 168) also hints at the nation's hypocrisy; in Roosevelt's pocket is a sheet of paper inscribed "Cuba" and "Philippines," a reminder of the United States' own imperial ambitions.

171
Le trust du gas (The gas trust), probably 1903
Rostro
No. 175
Lithograph (undivided back)

172
An American millionaire, about 1900
[Signature illegible]
Color lithograph (undivided back)

A controversy about the ownership and management of the Paris gas company erupted in the late winter and spring of 1903, when one group bidding for the municipal contract was rumored to be supported by John D. Rockefeller, the richest man in the world. This possibility of American control over a key French utility was made more

suspect by rumors of hidden assets and silent partners. During the first decade of the twentieth century, European cartoonists increasingly targeted the United States, often using bulging money bags as a symbol of the country's deep pockets.

173–176
Bowling kings, about 1911
Charles Naillod (French, 1876–1956)
Published in Paris by Cie. Brunswick; printed in Paris by Breger & Lang
Color lithographs (divided back)

The bowlers here are the crowned heads of Europe, each with the costume and physical attributes familiar from caricatures. In the 1890s bowling was transformed by standardized rules and new technology, such as the innovative rubber balls produced by the Brunswick company, which issued these cards. One card is stamped "Bowling à Magic City," suggesting it was used to promote a bowling alley at an amusement park that opened on the left bank of the Seine in 1911.

177–180
Looping the loop, before 1906
Elym
Published and printed in Paris by J.M.
Color lithographs (undivided back)

Popularized by a U.S. bicyclist known as "Diavolo" (he performed in a red costume with horns and a cape), the loop-the-loop became all the rage at circuses during the first decade of the twentieth century. Here, European rulers loop the loop on appropriate vehicles: a cannon for the bellicose Wilhelm II of Germany, a gondola for Italy's Victor Emmanuel III. Edward VII's hobbyhorse may refer both to his well-known love of the races and to his possession as a child of the first such toy in England.

181–182
Jack Johnson, about 1910
Photographed and printed in San Francisco by The Dana Studio, nos. Jo-6 and Jo-7
Real photographs on card stock (divided back)

These cards seem to have been shot as part of the publicity blitz that surrounded the heavyweight title bout between Jack Johnson and John Jeffries, in Reno, Nevada, on July 4, 1910. The fight, called, inevitably, the "Battle of the Century," was front-page news across the United States. Jeffries, who was white, had long refused to fight Johnson because of his race, and Johnson's victory set off a series of race riots throughout the country.

183–185
Elle se trotte toujours (*La Joconde*!) (She really gets around [*Mona Lisa*!]), about 1913
Printed by FC & Cie.
Real photograph and photolithographic collages (divided back)

When the *Mona Lisa* was stolen in 1911, speculation was rife about where she had gone. These cards hint at various possibilities. Out for a donkey ride on the Champs-Elysées? Shopping in the posh district near the Paris Opéra? Or perhaps on a trip to see the Pyramids with Arsène Lupin, a fictional gentleman-thief? Other cards from the series show her in front of London's Houses of Parliament and visiting the Statue of Liberty in New York. Those showing her in Paris were closest to the truth. The thief, Vicenzo Peruggia (a sometime employee of the Louvre), kept the painting for more than two years in a rented room before taking it to Italy, where he believed he would be celebrated for returning the painting to its homeland. Instead, he went to prison.

186
Zeppelin. Internationale Luftschiffahrt-Ausstellung Frankfurt a. M. 1909 (International aircraft exhibition at Frankfurt am Main 1909), 1909
H. Roth
Published in Rödelheim, Frankfurt am Main by Brieke & Roth
Color lithograph (divided back)

187
Zeppelin auf einer Spritztour nach Paris–London (Zeppelin on a Paris–London joyride), 1914

Hans Müller (German, 1879–1951?)
Published in Karlsruhe, Germany, by Geschwister Moos; printed in Karslruhe by Arthur Albrecht & Cie.
Color lithograph (divided back)

Ferdinand, Count Zeppelin, whose long-distance dirigible flights put Germany on the aviation map, was among the presiding heroes of the 1909 Frankfurt air show. Capable of long-distance travel, the eponymous zeppelins helped fuel growing alarm about Germany's imperial ambitions. These fears were confirmed when the zeppelin was used for aerial bombing during the First World War.

188
Wilbur Wright. Internationale Luftschiffahrt Ausstellung Frankfurt a. M. 1909 (International aircraft exhibition at Frankfurt am Main 1909), 1909
H. Roth
Published in Rödelheim, Frankfurt am Main, by Brieke & Roth
Color lithograph (divided back)

189
W. Wright. Un vol à l'americaine (W. Wright. Flight, American style), after 1903
Published in Paris by A-N Paris (Alfred Noyer Studio)
Model by César Giris (Cesare Giri) (Italian, worked in France, 1877–1941)
Real photograph on card stock (divided back)

Once Wilbur Wright successfully flew and landed his Flyer at the Aéro-Club de France, near Le Mans, in August 1908, he became a celebrity icon in Europe—the subject of many postcard images as well as countless news articles and even popular songs.

190
Econo Infrangibile lightbulbs, about 1910
Published in Berlin by Köhler, Spiller & Co.; printed in Bologna by E. Vecchi
Color lithograph (divided back)

The back of the card claims maximum efficiency and incomparable durability for the "unbreakable" (*infrangibile*) Econo bulb.

191
See figs. 201–202

192
See figs. 211–212

193
Une nouvelle étoile: La Métallique A.E.G. Record de l'économie (A new star: The Métallique A.E.G. Record efficiency), after 1908
Published in Paris by Stelmans
Color lithograph (divided back)

194
Bergman Lampe (Bergmann lightbulbs), about 1910
Carl Zander (German, born in 1872)
Printed in Germany
Color lithograph (divided back)

195
Philips Argenta, about 1923
Hans Oertle (German, 1897–1975)
Published by Philips
Color lithograph (divided back)

196
Lampe Philips (Philips lightbulbs), about 1909
Published by Philips
Color lithograph (divided back)

Cards for lightbulbs are a reminder that multinational corporations dominated the world of technology even in the early twentieth century. The very French-looking astronomer who catches sight of a new incandescent star hanging over Paris (fig. 193) is actually gazing at a German product. The bulb was made by Allgemeine Elektricitäts Gesellschaft, Germany's answer to General Electric. Similarly, the card for the Econo bulb (fig. 190) is directed at Italian consumers, but the company that produced the bulbs was German; and the radiating bands of color that captivate the young girl on the Philips Argenta card (fig. 195) were featured in advertising from the Netherlands to Croatia.

197
Elektr. Licht. Billiger als Petroleum (Electric light. Cheaper than petroleum), about 1910

Published in Berlin by the Geschäftsstelle für Elektrizitätsverwertung
Color lithograph (divided back)

198
Elektrisch Licht (Electric light), about 1910
Martin Lehmann-Steglitz (German, 1884–1949 or 1950) and Walter Lehmann-Steglitz (German, 1884–1921)
Color lithograph (divided back)

199–200
Westinghouse appliances, after 1914
Frederick Goss Cooper (American, 1883–1962)
Published in New York by Westinghouse Electric Company
Color lithographs (divided back)

201–202
Women using electric appliances, about 1936
Lawrence Sterne Stevens (American, 1884–1960)
Published in Brussels by the Union des Exploitations Électriques en Belgique (U.E.E.B.)
Color lithographs (divided back)

203
Ventilateur électrique (Electric fan), about 1930
Lawrence Sterne Stevens (American, 1884–1960)
Published in Brussels by the U.E.E.B
Color lithograph (divided back)

204
Marelli ventilatoren (Marelli fans), about 1930
Published in Bologna by ATLA
Color lithograph (divided back)

205–208
Courses automobiles (Car racing), about 1903
Fernand Fernel (Belgian, 1872–1934)
Color lithographs (undivided back)

Fernel often published his work in *Le rire* (The Laugh), one of the myriad satirical journals whose artists cross-pollinated with the world of postcards in turn-of-the-century Paris. Since these cars are clearly based on

actual models, it seems likely that Fernel worked from photographs, possibly news reports of the catastrophic Paris-to-Madrid road race of 1903.

209
Shell. Huile + essence = vitesse! (Shell. Oil + gas = speed!), about 1930
Published in Belgium by Polstobb
Color lithograph (divided back)

210
Shell. Essences, huiles (Shell gas and oil), about 1920
A.E.
Color lithograph (divided back)

211–212
Spidoléine oil, 1924
Published in Genoa, Italy, by Cimo & Co.
Color lithographs (divided back)

The motorcycle-racing circuit was well established by the 1920s; these cards celebrate races won in 1924 by motorcycles that used Spidoleine oil. Monet Goyon (fig. 192), A.J.S., and Condor were brands of motorcycles.

213
Deutscher Rundflug 1911. Überharzflug Halberstadt (German flight 1911. Flight over the Harz Mountains to Halberstadt), 1911
Richard Thomas
Published in Halberstadt, Germany, by Louis Koch
Color lithograph after woodcut original (divided back)

Early aviators often banded together to make aerial tours of a region. Billed as "the greatest aviation event" of its time, the first German cross-country flight took place in June and July 1911. The tour began with twelve planes and ended with only three, covering 1,850 kilometers (1,150 miles) in thirteen legs interspersed with air shows and competitions. Here, the pilots finish up the second-to-last leg, flying across the Harz mountain range.

214
Prinz-Heinrich Flug 10–17 Mai 1913 (Prince Heinrich flight), 1913

Ernst Riess
Published in Strassburg, Germany
Color lithograph after woodcut original (divided back)

Prince Heinrich of Prussia was an avid supporter of aviation and trained as a pilot. The flight that bore his name was an endurance run along the upper Rhine River. In 1913, Strassburg (now Strasbourg, France) was still part of Germany, which had wrested it from France in 1871, during the Franco-Prussian War.

215
Ostpreussischer Rundflug 9–14 August 1913 (East Prussian flight), 1913
H.W.
Published in Königsberg, Germany (now Kaliningrad, Russia), by H. Schwarz
Color lithograph after woodcut original (divided back)

This card advertises a five-day aerial excursion around East Prussia, the area along the Baltic Sea that Germany would cede to Poland and Russia after World War II.

216
Wings! Madison Square Garden and the 69th Regiment Armory. Aeronautical Exposition March 1st to 15th, 1919
John E. Sheridan (American, 1880–1948)
Published in New York
Chromolithograph (divided back)

World War I brought rapid technical advancement to airplanes. The 1919 aeronautical exposition in New York marked the first time that many of the new machines of the war years were put on full view. The show included some new civilian planes as well, including a number of "aerial limousines" with "elaborate fixtures and numerous comforts for those who desire to fly rather than ride from place to place."

217
Great Aeronautics Exhibition, 1934
Published in Kanazawa, Japan, by the Miyaichi Daimaru department store
Photolithograph with metallic ink (divided back)

The exhibition was held October 1–10 in the department store's fifth-floor exhibition hall and was sponsored by the Ministry of Transportation and Communications, the Imperial Aeronautics Association, and Japan Air Freight, Inc.

218
The sky, the sea—places where men go, probably before 1941
Published in Japan
Color lithograph with metallic ink
(divided back)

219
Air France. Muchas felicidades 1935
(Air France. Best wishes for 1935), 1934
Printed in Argentina
Color lithograph (divided back)

Though the drawing appears stylized, it is a reasonably faithful rendering of the first Air France plane on the Paris–South America mail run: the Couzinet 70 Arc-en-ciel (Rainbow). Air France began service on the route in late 1933, traveling by way of Dakar, Senegal. The trip took nearly a week.

220
Via Condor. Feliz navidad y prospero año nuevo. (Air Condor. Merry Christmas and Happy New Year.), 1936
Published in Argentina
Color lithograph with metallic ink
(divided back)

Transatlantic airmail was an object of imperial competition. Intended to challenge France's monopoly on the run, the Condor service was operated by a Brazilian company that worked with Germany's Lufthansa. This holiday card could be sent with reduced postage on flights in December and January.

221
Ibis. MAK π 100, about 1930
De Robertis
Published in Naples by Manzoni & de Luccia
Color lithograph (divided back)

222
MAK π 100. 1000, about 1930
[Signature illegible]
Published in Naples by Manzoni & de Luccia
Color lithograph (divided back)

Despite the airplanes that zip through the air, these cards actually celebrate an event on the ground. MAK Pi is, effectively, the homecoming celebration for the Italian military academies, held one hundred days before graduation.

223
Taliedo. Grande giornata aviatoria, 8 luglio 1934, ore 16.30 (Taliedo. Great aviation day, 8 July 1934, 4:30 p.m.), 1934
N. Longo (?)
Published in Milan by G. Landsmans
Color lithograph (divided back)

Taliedo was Milan's first airport, a modest establishment rather grandly billed as "Italy's Aerodrome" when it was built at the end of one of the city's streetcar lines around 1910. Although the design appears quite abstract, it is based on forms seen from the air: even the wavy line above the word Taliedo mimics the roofline of the airport's main sheds.

224
Roma–Chicago–New York–Roma. Crociera aerea del Decennale 1933–XI (Rome–Chicago–New York–Rome. Decennial air cruise), 1933
Marcello Dudovich (Italian, 1878–1962)
Published in Milan by I.G.A.P.
Color lithograph (divided back)

225
Crociera aerea del Decennale 1933–XI (Decennial air cruise), 1933
Luigi Martinati (Italian, 1893–1983)
Published in Milan by I.G.A.P. (Navarra?)
Color lithograph (divided back)

The XI in the date on these cards refers to year eleven of Mussolini's Fascist government.

226
Luftschiff "Graf Zeppelin" benutzt ausschliesslich Veedol Motorenoel (The airship *Graf Zeppelin* uses Veedol motor oil exclusively), about 1931
Photolithograph with metallic paint
(divided back)

227
The zeppelin hall at Rhein-Main airport, about 1935
Published in Frankfurt am Main by Deutsche Zeppelin-Reederei
Real photograph on card stock (divided back)

Inspired by Ferdinand, Count Zeppelin (see figs. 186–187), who devoted his career to developing lighter-than-air flight, Germany invested more resources and effort in building a commercially viable fleet of such aircraft than any other nation. From the late 1920s until the mid-1930s, ever-larger airships served as German calling cards around the world. Nearly 237 meters (776 feet) long, the *Graf Zeppelin* made hundreds of regularly scheduled flights to South America in the 1930s.

228
An actual photo of the *Hindenburg* disaster. Lakehurst, N.J., May 6th, 1937
Published in Rutherford, N.J., by The Garraway Company
Real photograph on card stock (divided back)

The Garraway Company's primary business was making postcards for local clients. Here the company got hold of one of the iconic images of the twentieth century.

229
See figs. 235–236

230
Michelin tires. C. L. & Theo. Bering Jr. Inc., Houston, Texas, about 1910
Published in Houston
Real photograph on card stock (divided back)

231–232
Falstaff beer, about 1909
Published in the United States for William J. Lemp Brewing Co.
Real photographs on card stock
(divided back)

Based in Saint Louis, Lemp was one of the leading brewers in the United States around the turn of the century. Falstaff, launched in June 1899, quickly became Lemp's leading brand.

233
Gancia Asti Spumante, 1922
Leonetto Cappiello (Italian, 1875–1942)
Published in Paris and Turin by Devambez
Color lithograph (divided back)

234
Omega watches, about 1920
Leonetto Cappiello (Italian, 1875–1942)
Published in Paris by Établissements Vercasson
Color lithograph, textured (divided back)

235–236
Talmone chocolate, about 1901
Franz Laskoff (Franciszek Laskowski)
(Polish, worked in Italy, 1869–1918)
Published in Milan by Officine Grafiche Ricordi & Company
Color lithographs (undivided back)

In the years around 1900, Talmone, based in Turin, was Italy's largest chocolate company. It maintained grand and elegant art nouveau cafés in Turin and Milan.

237–239
Mele department stores, about 1900
Probably Aleardo Villa (Italian, 1865–1906)
Published in Milan by Officine Grafiche Ricordi & Company
Color lithographs (undivided back)

These cards were meant as seductive keepsakes, but they were also meant to lure customers. Even so, the artist may not have expected the phrase "massimo buon mercato" (roughly "very best deals") to accompany the frank and seductive stare of the blond woman in fig. 238.

240
Michelin tires, about 1908
Carlo Biscaretti di Ruffia (Italian, 1879–1959)
Published by Agenzia italiana dei Pneumatici Michelin; printed in Milan by Rinascenza Grafica
Color lithograph (divided back)

The multitalented Biscaretti designed cars as well as illustrations and advertisements for Michelin's monthly Italian magazine. His take on Bibendum, the Michelin Man, was unusually worldly and ironic. In addition to this tête-à-tête with historical world leaders, other illustrations show him listening to a poet recounting his glories in the sing-songy *terza rima* associated with Dante's *Divine Comedy* and oh-so-modestly receiving thousands of fan letters.

241
Michelin tires, about 1910
Winters
Published in Haarlem, the Netherlands, by M. A. Jacobson
Color lithograph (divided back)

242–244
Continental Pneumatic, about 1900
Some signed G.L.
Some published in Hannover, Germany, by Edler & Krische (for the United States market)
Color lithographs (undivided back)

245
La Sartotecnica, about 1931
Federico Seneca (Italian, 1891–1975)
Printed in Italy by Pizzi & Pizio
Color lithograph (divided back)

Catalogues for Sartotecnica, a Milanese supply house for tailors, were distributed throughout Italy. The back of this card features an excerpt from the *Song of the Sartotecnica*, "broadcast by radio on all the Italian radio stations":

If you go to the tailor, my good sir,
Pay close attention and be sure to order
The best fabrics of the finest wool,
The Sartotecnica alone will do!
The "sample book," The Sartotecnica,
Is the very handbook for the gentleman of style.

246
Danois cheese, about 1930
T. Rayez
Printed in Brussels by "Soc. Calendar" P. Meur
Color lithograph (divided back)

247
Bitter Campari (Campari bitters), 1921
Leonetto Cappiello (Italian, 1875–1942)
Published in Italy
Color lithograph (divided back)

248
Las conservas Albo son las mejores
(Albo preserves are the best), about 1930
Color lithograph (divided back)

Albo remains one of Spain's leading purveyors of tinned fish.

249–252
Rochefort wallpapers, about 1925
Published in Paris by Papiers Peints Rochefort; printed in Nancy, France, by Arts Graphiques
Color lithographs with metallic ink (divided back)

253
Carpano vermouth, about 1930?
Published in Italy by Studio Testa; printed in Milan by Arti Grafiche Fratelli Pirovano
Color lithograph (divided back)

254
Borsalino hats, about 1936
Published in Milan and Rome by Bertieri
Color lithograph (divided back)

This card for Borsalino (founded in 1887 and still in business) neatly threads the needle of creating a striking graphic statement and showing a product faithfully. The design is dominated by the x-man, but the hat he holds is actually a photograph.

255–256
Madeleine Vionnet. Robes, Manteaux, Fourrures (Madeleine Vionnet. Gowns, coats, furs), 1922
Thayaht (Ernesto Michahelles) (Italian, 1893–1959)

Published in France by Coquemer
Color lithographs (divided back)

Madeleine Vionnet and Thayaht's close artistic relationship began in 1919. Questioned about her collaborations with illustrators, the couturier stated that "the illustrator's imagination may be rich in terms of the colors, arrangements and combinations of fabric, but he doesn't understand the 'essence' of the fabric . . . The illustrator, therefore, needs to work with a couturier."

These cards sell the modern art of selling—and show how deeply ingrained modernist styles had become in Germany during the 1920s. The close-ups, the cropped photographs, and the almost cinematic approach to drawing attention to the telling detail exemplify the up-to-date advertising and design the firm could offer.

The Deutscher Schulverein (German School Association) was a major postcard publisher in Vienna, commissioning at least 160 artists to produce cards with German nationalist sentiments. Moser's cards belong to a series of graphic works he created after resigning from the Wiener Werkstätte in 1907, when he developed a new interest in figurative art.

The Israelite House of David, a millenarian religious community founded in 1903 in Benton Harbor, Michigan, originally promoted baseball as a leisure activity for its members. The team began playing more competitively around 1915 and by 1920 was playing against semipro teams, combining the sport with fundraising and preaching activities. The players' long hair and beards were dictated by the group's doctrines.

Founded in 1896, the Hannover Sport-Club, primarily a soccer club, was put in charge of a week of sports festivals held to celebrate the inauguration of the city's new town hall.

From its origins in mid-nineteenth-century England, soccer became a Europe-wide phenomenon by the early twentieth century. Here, success in the sport is tied to smoking Diana cigarettes: "Each goal that I shoot is impossible to defend, because I come to the game with Diana."

282
Berliner Sport-Club (Berlin Sports Club),
about 1925
Ludwig Hohlwein (German, 1874–1949)
Printed in Munich by Graphia

The primary interest of the Berliner Sport-
Club, founded in 1899, was track and field.
Hohlwein was Germany's leading poster
designer in the early twentieth century; his
signature style, with sharply designed figural
forms, emphasized the virile national body.
He later became a propagandist for Hitler's
Germany (see figs. 301–302).

283–284
Golf and croquet from a series showing
women in fashionable sportswear, about 1910
Melanie (Mela) Koehler (Austrian, 1885–1960)
Published in Vienna by B.K.W.
Color lithographs (divided back)

285–286
Continental lawn-tennis balls, about 1900
Published in Hannover, Germany, by the
Continental-Caoutchouc und Gutta-Percha
Compagnie; printed in Hannover by Edler
& Krische
Color lithographs (divided back)

287–290
From the series Jeux Olympiques Paris 1924
(Olympic Games, Paris), 1924
E. Blanche
Color lithographs (divided back)

In the mid-1920s, the Paris art world again
became enamored of the idea of classical
order and the art of ancient Greece and
Rome. As the Olympics were themselves a
revival of antiquity, this artist marked the
games with cards inspired by ancient Athenian
vase paintings—even for sports without an
ancient precedent, such as rugby and tennis.

291–292
Lawn-tennis match and Fussball Wettspiel
(Football sweepstakes), about 1930?
Color lithographs (divided back)

293–294
Épée (Fencing) and Boxe (Boxing) from the
series Jeux Olympiques Paris 1924 (Olympic
Games, Paris), 1924
H. L. Roowy
Printed in Paris by Parisienne
Color lithographs (divided back)

295–298
RSI Spartakiada 1928 Moskva (RSI
Spartakiada, Moscow), 1928
Gustavs Klucis (Latvian, 1895–1944)
Published in Moscow by RSI—Red Sport
International
Photolithograph collages (divided back)

Sports and fitness were important to Soviet
ideology, but the Soviet Union considered the
Olympic Games too closely tied to capitalist
and imperial power structures and did not
participate until 1952. Instead, Red Sports
International (part of the Communist
International, or Comintern) organized a
parallel competition that took its name
from Spartacus, leader of a slave revolt in
ancient Rome. Designed when the Soviet
Union was still open to artistic experimentation, these energetic cards are dedicated to
"the unity of worker-athletes of the world!"

299–300
III. středoškolské hry Praha 1932 (Third
Intercollegiate Games, Prague), 1932
Jiři Taufer (Czech, 1911–1986)
Lithographs (divided back)

Taufer, who later became a poet and a
communist activist, designed these postcards
when he was still a student. They were made
for athletic competitions held to commemo-
rate the founding of the Sokol movement,
which promoted the physical, moral, and intellectual development of Slavic youth and reinforced Czech national identity.

301
Deutsche Lufthansa, 1936
Ludwig Hohlwein (German, 1874–1949)
Printed in Germany by Deutsche Lufthansa
A.G.
Color lithograph (divided back)

302
Deutschland 1936. IV Olympische Winter-
spiele. Garmisch-Partenkirchen. 6–16 Februar
1936 (Germany 1936. Fourth Winter
Olympics. Garmisch-Partenkirchen. 6–16
February), 1936
Ludwig Hohlwein (German, 1874–1949)
Published in Germany
Color lithograph (divided back)

303
Olympia 1936. Die erste Gold-Medaille für
Deutschland. Sieger-Ehrung (1936 Olympics.
The first gold medal for Germany. Award
ceremony), 1936
Printed in Munich by Hoffmann (Heinrich
Hoffmann)
Real photograph on card stock (divided back)

This card commemorates the first German
gold medal at the Berlin Olympics, in the
women's javelin event; the silver medal also
went to a German athlete. Newsreel footage
shows that the medal presentation was staged
as a photo opportunity for Adolf Hitler and
Joseph Goebbels, who were standing near
the podium.

304
Oneglia. Gli oli d'oliva P. Sasso e Figli di
Oneglia sono gli unici perfetti (Oneglia.
The olive oils of P. Sasso and Sons of Oneglia
are the only perfect ones), about 1900
Published in Oneglia, Italy, by P. Sasso e Figli;
printed in Milan by Gabriele Chiattone
Color lithograph (undivided back)

305
Sunshine holidays to Algiers & Genoa by
Nederland Royal Mail Line, about 1929
Published in the Netherlands by Stoomvaart
Maatschappij Nederland
Color lithograph (divided back)

306
Skegness is so bracing, about 1908
John Hassall (English, 1868–1948)
From the series Celesque
Published in London and Detroit by The
Photochrom Co. Ltd.; printed in England
Color lithograph (divided back)

Hassall invented his jolly fisherman for a poster that marked the opening of the Great Northern Railway's connection between London and the North Sea town of Skegness. The image inspired the sender of this card to whimsy during a restorative visit to the seaside in August 1913: "Dear Doctor, I can't claim to feel like the fisherman here depicted, but am going along alright."

307
Spoorwegen-Staatsspoor in Nederland (Netherlands State Railways), about 1900
Published in Amsterdam by Faddegon & Co.
Color lithograph (divided back)

308–309
Menu postcards for the Red Star Line, 1905
Probably Henri Cassiers (Belgian, 1858–1944)
Published in Brussels by Lith. O. de Rycker
Color lithographs (undivided back)

Cards like these from the S. S. *Zeeland* did double duty. Each day, the ship's restaurant printed the dinner menu on the lower portion; when the meal was finished, the passenger could tear the top part off along a perforation and send it as a postcard.

310–311
R.M.S. *Mauretania* and R.M.S. *Aquitania*, 1922
Published in the United States by A. & P., no. 47850
Color lithographs (divided back)

In the 1920s, the British steamship company Cunard boasted a fleet of more than fifteen liners, but the line's reputation rested largely on the "big three:" the *Aquitania*, *Mauretania*, and *Berengaria*. These postcards reproduce illustrations from brochures issued around 1922, just after the *Mauretania* underwent a major overhaul.

312–313
The Hamburg–South America liner *Cap Arcona*, after 1927
Published in Hamburg by Hamburg-Südamerikanische Dampfschifffahrts-Gesellschaft

Real photographs on card stock (divided back)

Launched in 1927, the *Cap Arcona* was built for the busy run from Hamburg to Brazil and Argentina. The fifteen-day voyage gave the passengers much time for recreation.

314
Grand hôtel l'océan. La panne-bains près d'Ostende Belgique (Grand Hotel Ocean. Beach tennis near Ostend, Belgium), about 1900
Published in Bruges, Belgium, by La Lithographie Artistique, no. 2926
Color lithograph (divided back)

This postcard, which reproduces a poster for the hotel, leaves little room for the sender's message. The back is taken up entirely with the hotel's schedule of room rates for the summer. Prices were highest in August, but the hotel offered free parking and seawall access. Call at telephone number "1."

315
La panne-bains (Beach tennis), about 1900
Printed in Brussels by Lith. J. Goffin, fils
Color lithograph (divided back)

316
Au bain (Bathing), about 1900
Published in France by Louis Lévy et fils, no. 5058
Photolithograph (divided back)

317
Souvenir de Blankenberghe (Souvenir of Blankenberghe), about 1900
Published in Brussels by A. Dohmen, no. 528
Photolithograph (divided back)

318
Les plages belges. Retour du bain (The Belgian beaches. Back from bathing), about 1900
Published in Brussels by Th. van den Heuvel, no. 111
Photolithograph (divided back)

Blanche McManus described turn-of-the-century bathing in Belgium in *The American Woman Abroad* (1911): "One bathes here exclusively from the bathing machine, a little house on wheels; you enter, a man hitches a horse, and the 'machine' is taken on the run down into the surf. The horse and driver go back to dry land while you undress and step down into the water as if out of your own front door. You enter again and dress, and, at a prearranged time, the horse and man come and drag the 'machine' out again."

319–320
Hotel New Grand, Yokohama, Japan, about 1920
Color lithographs with silver metallic paint (divided back)

321
Visit Cuba. So near and yet so foreign. 90 miles from Key West, 1930s
Conrado Walter Massaguer (Cuban, 1889–1965)
Published by the Cuban Tourist Commission; printed in Chicago by Genuine Curteich-Chicago, C.T. Art-Colortone, no. IB-H629
Color lithograph on linen-textured card stock

322
Nice l'été. Quelles bonnes vacances! (Nice in the summer. What a great vacation!)
ER
Published in Nice, France, by l'Association Syndicale des Hôteliers de Nice; printed in Nice by Sté. Gle
Color lithograph (divided back)

323
Riva, about 1900
Published by the Società Anonima per Azioni Impresa di Navigazione sul Lago di Garda; printed in Milan by Gabriele Chiattone
Color lithograph (undivided back)

324
Camogli, Riviera di levante (Camogli, Italian Riviera), about 1900
Published in Oneglia, Italy, by P. Sasso e Figli; printed in Milan by Officine d'arti grafiche Chiattone
Color lithograph (divided back)

The card of the town of Camogli doubles as an advertisement for Sasso olive oil, which published the series (see also fig. 304).

325
Hotel Nettuno, Pisa, about 1910
Tombi
Published in Como, Italy, by Casartelli
Color lithograph (divided back)

The image selected by a hotel could literally travel the world, so it was important to be consistent. The Hotel Nettuno used this same romantic scene of Pisa's leaning tower on postcards, posters, and luggage tags, though it is doubtful any room in the hotel commanded this particular view.

326
Abbazia, 1936
Printed in Udine, Italy, by Grafiche Chiesa
Color lithograph (divided back)

Now in Croatia and called Opatija, the Adriatic coast town of Abbazia had been part of the Austro-Hungarian empire and was assigned to Italy after World War I. That link to Central Europe may explain the German advertisement on the back of this card, promoting the town's second operetta festival, which featured a retrospective of works by the Hungarian-Viennese composer Emmerich Kálmán.

327–330
Rio de Janeiro, 1934
Manuel Móra (Brazilian, born in Portugal, 1884–1956)
Published in Rio de Janeiro by the Departamento de Turismo de municipalidade do Rio de Janeiro
Color lithographs (divided back)

In the 1920s and 1930s, Rio de Janeiro emerged as one of the most fashionable destinations in the Americas. To appeal to the city's increasingly international clientele, in 1934 Rio's department of tourism commissioned a series of eight postcards, each featuring a lovely young woman of a different nationality.

331
Advance Zephyrs between Chicago and Denver. Streamlined. Diesel-powered. Built of stainless steel. 1034 miles overnight, 1934
Published in the United States by the Burlington and Quincy Railroad
Color lithograph with silver metallic ink (divided back)

Printed to celebrate the new service, this card includes a "stop press" update in red on the back: "the ADVANCE DENVER ZEPHYRS have reached their terminals exactly 'On Time' for 40 consecutive days."

332
20th Century Limited. New York—16 hours—Chicago, via the Water Level route, 1938
Published in the United States by the New York Central Railroad
Color lithograph (divided back)

Many collectors prefer cards that are "postally unused," but occasionally a used card has special resonance. This advertisement for "the last word in streamlined beauty" was stamped by the railroad to announce the first run of the new train. The sender, presumably a passenger, sent it off to an address in Dunedin, New Zealand. It cost two cents to mail.

333
110 mile-per-hour Union Pacific streamlined passenger train, about 1935
Published in the United States
Real photograph on card stock (divided back)

334–335
Calmante Rosa, about 1935
Color lithographs (divided back)

"In treno?" (On a train?) or "In automobile?" (In a car?). Apparently, Calmante Rosa, or "soothing pink," is appropriate anywhere—at least anywhere a dapper traveler might need a remedy for motion sickness.

336
Normandie. Le Havre, after 1935
Ch. Meunier (photographer)
12-postcard booklet published by G. Boüan
Cover: color lithograph; postcards: photo-lithographs (divided back)

337
Normandie. Compagnie Générale Transatlantique, 1938
20-postcard booklet published in Strasbourg by Cie. des Arts Photomécaniques Schiltigheim
Cover: color lithograph; postcards: photo-lithographs (divided back)

338–341
Valdura products at the Century of Progress Exposition, 1933
Published in Chicago by American Asphalt Paint Company
Color lithographs, some with gold or sliver metallic paint (divided back)

Chicago's Century of Progress Exposition may have been the most carefully planned of all World's Fairs. The organizers even hired the theater designer Joseph Urban to create a color palette for the fair that would convey a sense of futuristic harmony. The American Asphalt Paint Company won the paint contract and used the opportunity to promote their Valdura brand. The company also used the images on these postcards in an extensively annotated promotional brochure called *Color and Protection.*

342–344
Prima mostra triennale delle terre italiane d'oltremare (First triennial exhibition of the Italian overseas territories), 1940
Cella
Published in Naples by F. Raimondi
Color lithographs (divided back)

These cards were issued to promote the signage and wayfinding system at a 1940 exhibition celebrating the products and accomplishments of Italy's African colonies. This first triennial exposition of Italian imperialism was, of course, also the last.

In this card from the beginning of the war, the black-and-yellow flag represents the Austrian Hapsburg Empire, while the black-white-red flag stands for Germany—the "united forces" of the inscription.

Aerial warfare was a new phenomenon in World War I. Here, an alarmed French soldier, wearing a useless dress sword, climbs the Eiffel Tower to wave a reminder at the German aviators: "Warning! Bomb-throwing strictly prohibited!" The bombs fly anyway.

These cards are based on cartoons from the English magazine *The Bystander*, whose November 4, 1914, issue included a spread comparing the two armies to a pair of "scientific wrestlers." The magazine's sequence ends on October 26, when the first Battle of Ypres was still in full fury; the postcards add a "knockout": the November 10 Battle of Bixschoote (or Langemarck).

Georgi was one of seven artists Hermann Bahlsen commissioned to design postcards at the beginning of World War I for the Feldpost, the German army postal service, which provided free mail service to soldiers. Each of Georgi's alert and heroic soldiers carries a package of Bahlsen's Leibniz cookies. It is unclear whether Bahlsen's *Feldpostkarten* were sold, like the postcards issued by the Red Cross, or given away with purchases of cookies.

The "English disease" is both a sneering reference to syphilis and an allusion to Germany's perception that Britain depended too much on naval power. John Bull stands on shoes made of destroyers and tries to protect himself with a very English umbrella while a German zeppelin floats above, neatly marked "Made in Germany."

371

John Bull on his little ships, about 1914
W.S. or T.S.
Published by W.B.S.S. or S.S.W.B., no. 583
Color lithograph (divided back)

High above England,
German zeppelins prowl the air:
John Bull sits out on the little ships
and opens his umbrella to protect himself.

372

Kaiser Wilhelm, 1914–17
T.
Published and printed in Saint Petersburg by Bussel & Knoring
Color lithograph (divided back)

"Like an out-of-his mind satyr, Wilhelm, the biggest fool of them all, in the heat of madness wants to flood the entire world with blood."

373

Neron nashikh dney (The Nero of our times), 1914–17
T.
Published and printed in Saint Petersburg by Bussel & Knoring
Color lithograph (divided back)

This card was printed on the same sheet as the previous one. Careless trimming left part of the design for this card at the bottom of the other.

374–375

German armaments, 1915 and 1916
Carl Otto Czeschka (Austrian, 1878–1960)
Published in Hannover, Germany, by H. Bahlsens Keks Fabrik
Color lithographs (divided back)

Like figs. 349 and 368–369, these cards were issued by the Bahlsen cookie company as *Feldpostkarten*. While most Bahlsen cards feature soldiers carrying packages of Leibniz cookies, Czeschka's celebrate the armaments that represented German military might. Despite being issued for use by soldiers at the front, the six-card set was aimed at the collectors' market as well; it came with a cover, like artists' cards.

376–377

Die Herren der Lüfte (Masters of the air) and Unsere Marine (Our navy) from the series Künstler Kriegs (War artist), about 1914
Heinrich (Heinz) Keune (German, 1881–1946)
Published in Hannover, Germany, by J. C König & Ebhardt
Color lithographs (divided back)

These cards appeared very early in the war, when the civilian economy had not yet been severely disrupted. Produced with high-quality paper and printing, they were also distributed in the January–February 1915 issue of *Das Plakat*, the Berlin journal for poster collectors.

378

"Daddy, what did *you* do in the Great War?" 1916
Savile Lumley (British, 1876–about 1950)
Printed in Saint Petersburg by Union Printing House
Color lithograph (divided back)

"I have often laughed to think of that recruiting poster, 'What did you do in the Great War, daddy?' (a child is asking this question of its

shame-stricken father), and of all the men who must have been lured into the army by just that poster and afterwards despised by their children for not being Conscientious Objectors" (George Orwell, "My Country, Right or Left," 1940). It is testament to the power of an image that it can remain controversial after two decades.

379

Women of Britain say—"Go!" 1916 (designed 1915)
E. V. Kealey
Printed in Saint Petersburg by Union Printing House
Color lithograph (divided back)

Though this image is British, the card is Russian. Along with the previous card, it was printed in Saint Petersburg on the occasion of the 1916 exhibition *British Posters of the Great War*.

380

"You are the man I want," about 1915
Published and printed in London by The Regent Publishing Co., Ltd.
Color lithograph (divided back)

The man who wants you is Herbert, 1st Earl Kitchener, a pivotal figure in the Boer War, Commander-in-Chief of Britain's army in India from 1902 to 1909, Consul-General in British-dominated Egypt, and Secretary of State for War from 1914 until his death on a ship sunk by a German mine in 1916. In other words, the man who wants you is the very embodiment of the British Empire, which in 1915 was still the world-bestriding colossus upon which the sun never set.

Details

Page 1: fig. 253; pp. 2–3: fig. 293; pp. 4–5: fig. 36; p. 6: fig. 98; p. 8: fig. 249; pp. 272–73: fig. 11; p. 274: fig. 33; p. 294: fig. 103

ACKNOWLEDGMENTS

A book and exhibition like *The Postcard Age* inevitably involve a large and varied cast. We are tremendously grateful to all those who helped keep this project moving forward. They have provided clarity, advice, and solace, and saved us from many an embarrassing mistake; any remaining errors (and we are sure there are many) remain ours alone.

In New York and beyond, we owe debts, both scholarly and personal, to many, especially Emily Braun, Anna Jozefacka, Jocelyn Elliott, Luise Mahler, Anya Pantuyeva, Anna Indych-López, Alice Momm, Juliana Kreinik, Peter Dalton, Jonathan Mogul, Lori Canter, Catilin Dietze, Jeanie Janiro, Joan Krupskas, Michelle Sampaio, Lisa Somar, Margaret Stewart, Ben Stone, Terry Shargel, Antonella Pelizzari, Tara Zanardi, Janis Staggs, Eatira Solomon, and Nelida Valmoria. Many people in the worldwide network of poster and postcard scholars have helped greatly, and we owe debts of various kinds to Jack Rennert, Bob Bogdan, Dennis Goreham, Douglas Wayne, John and Ann Payne, Bruno de Perthuis, and Francis Gresse.

In Boston, the Museum of Fine Arts is home to a remarkable team that seems, over and over again, to make miracles happen. The book you hold would literally not exist without the efforts and patience of Jennifer Snodgrass, Emiko Usui, Terry McAweeney, Anna Barnet, Chris DiPietro, John Woolf, and Susan Marsh. The exhibition itself was the work of more hands than can be named, but key among them are Virginia Durruty, who provided an exciting and visionary design, and Lawrence Gibbons and his crew, who rendered that design in three dimensions. The graphics and words on the wall were the work of Marlene Tosca, Adam Tessier, Neal Johnson, Dustin Williams, and Nick Pioggia. Alton Davis's lighting made sure that we could actually see the cards as they were expertly examined, mounted, and treated by Nell Gould, Katrina Newbury, Saudra B. Lane Associate Conservator, Annette Manick, Albert Lewis, and Gail English. Jill Kennedy-Kernohan and Linda Pulliam helped guarantee that the cards arrived safely and were carefully accounted for. Quinn Corte, Chris Newth, and, above all, Gillian Fruh kept the whole process running with exemplary efficiency and good will.

Christraud Geary, Teel Senior Curator of African and Oceanic Art, and Anne Nishimura Morse, William and Helen Pounds Senior Curator of Japanese Art, provided much advice on postcards and museums in general. Amelia Kantrovitz made sure that the press near and far knew of *The Postcard Age*. And throughout the year, Carla Chrisfield and the staff of the Department of Prints, Drawings, and Photographs at the Museum of Fine Arts, have lent nearly unbounded affection and support.

Above all, we offer thanks to three people without whom *The Postcard Age* would have been impossible. Katie Getchell, Deputy Director, Museum of Fine Arts, has been an unfailing friend and support throughout the years and worked tirelessly to bring this project to fruition. Malcolm Rogers, Ann and Graham Gund Director, had the imagination and vision to understand the importance of the Lauder Archive to the MFA and led the campaign to bring it here. Lastly, we thank Leonard A. Lauder himself, who caught the postcard bug early and has helped spread it far and wide. He has been collaborator, adviser, enthusiast, goad, and wise resource, and for that we are most grateful, indeed.

L.K. AND B.W.

MFA Publications
Museum of Fine Arts, Boston
465 Huntington Avenue
Boston, Massachusetts 02115
www.mfa.org/publications

Published in conjunction with the exhibition
The Postcard Age, organized by the Museum
of Fine Arts, Boston, in the Lois B. and
Michael K. Torf Gallery, from October 24,
2012, to April 14, 2013.

Generous support for this exhibition and
publication was provided by the American
Art Foundation.

ISBN 978-0-87846-781-5 (hardcover)
ISBN 978-0-87846-787-7 (softcover)

Library of Congress Control Number:
2012937502

The Museum of Fine Arts, Boston, is a
nonprofit institution devoted to the promo-
tion and appreciation of the creative arts.
The Museum endeavors to respect the copy-
rights of all authors and creators in a manner
consistent with its nonprofit educational
mission. If you feel any material has been
included in this publication improperly,
please contact the Department of Rights
and Licensing at 617 267 9300, or by mail
at the above address.

While the objects in this publication necessarily represent only a small portion of the
MFA's holdings, the Museum is proud to
be a leader within the American museum
community in sharing the objects in its collection via its website. Currently, information
about more than 330,000 objects is available
to the public worldwide. To learn more
about the MFA's collections, including prove-
nance, publication, and exhibition history,
kindly visit *www.mfa.org/collections*.

For a complete listing of MFA publications,
please contact the publisher at the above
address, or call 617 369 3438.

All illustrations in this book were scanned
by Jocelyn Elliott and Anna Jozefacka unless
otherwise noted.

Edited by Jennifer Snodgrass
Proofread by Peg Anderson
Designed by Susan Marsh
Typeset in Gill Sans with Neutraface display
by Tina Henderson
Produced by Terry McAweeney
Production assistance by Anna Barnet
Printed on 135 gsm GardaPat Kiara
Printed and bound at Graphicom,
Verona, Italy

Available through ARTBOOK | D.A.P.
155 Sixth Avenue, 2nd floor
New York, New York 10013
Tel.: 212 627 1999 | Fax: 212 627 9484

FIRST EDITION

Printed and bound in Italy

This book was printed on acid-free paper.